Contents

Chapter 1

Introduction

The presence of American forces overseas is one of the most profound symbols of the U.S. commitments to allies and friends. . . . To contend with uncertainty and to meet the many security challenges we face, the United States will require bases and stations within and beyond Western Europe and Northeast Asia, as well as temporary access arrangements for the long-distance deployment of U.S. forces.

—*The National Security Strategy*
September 2002

The National Security Strategy (NSS) highlights the importance of overseas bases in advancing US national security objectives. Overseas bases have been a key component of US national security for decades and remain important for many strategic, operational, and tactical reasons. Strategically, overseas bases symbolize US commitment to our allies, signal credibility and capability to potential adversaries, represent US global influence, and create flexible policy options for political leaders. Operationally, overseas bases allow the United States to project power more efficiently into remote regions of the world, offer a greater diversity of military options to call upon in times of crisis, provide opportunities for foreign military cooperation and coalition building, and, most importantly, give the United States staging areas for high-intensity operations during prolonged conflicts. The tactical value of overseas bases cannot be overstated. They provide fixed, high-capacity locations from which to conduct operations closer to the source of conflict, increase aircraft sortie generation, greatly increase the endurance of US forces in a region, and provide key logistical nodes for resupply in a protracted conflict.

Future adversaries bent on regional aggression will seek to deny the US military by employing antiaccess strategies. Antiaccess strategies consist of geopolitical and threat-based measures taken to deny US power-projection capabilities prior to force application. Adversaries will likely employ antiaccess strategies based on the simple fact that US forces must overcome time, distance, and political constraints in order to influence global events—US strategies depend on getting close by using overseas bases. Hence, adversaries will attempt to deny US power projections through diplomatic coercion and propaganda. These efforts, which can involve either the promise of future punishments or rewards, will focus on preventing in-theater nations from allowing seaborne, land-based, or overflight access to US military forces. Additionally, adversaries will rigorously pursue military means to deny US military forces access to overseas regions. The ability to effectively counter the emerging antiaccess problem will significantly enhance US ability to project national will and power and protect our troops and allies with a strong offensive capability in a variety of situations. Any

1

antiaccess answer needs to offer a balanced and comprehensive approach that will strengthen the combat capability of all US military services.

Nowhere does this antiaccess capability grow more problematic than in the Pacific Rim, an area that already possesses a daunting antiaccess geography. In addition to the vast distances, primarily over ocean, several political flash points exist. These include Taiwan, Korea, Indonesia, and the Spratly Islands. Several potentially volatile nations, including China, India, Russia, Korea, Indonesia, Malaysia, and Japan, could take dramatic turns that could affect the strategic interests of the United States. In particular, the possible emergence of China as a regional belligerent peer looms large.

The potential emergence of China as a near-peer competitor in the Pacific Rim provides a focal point to address antiaccess issues in the region. Many defense analysts in the United States believe that China represents the most likely competitor to the United States for regional influence in the Pacific Rim in the future.[1] Over the past decade, China's economic growth has increased tremendously. With the influx of economic prosperity, China has attempted to significantly upgrade its military capabilities. For air defense, it purchased double-digit surface-to-air missiles (SAM)—SA-10s and SA-12s—and third-generation modern fighters such as SU-27s from Russia. Additionally, China developed increased antiaccess capabilities. These antiaccess capabilities include weapons of mass destruction (WMD) and advanced conventional weapons such as ballistic and surface-to-surface cruise missiles, antiship missiles, sea mines, and diesel submarines. With this increase in capabilities, China has begun to flex its muscles with an eye toward reclaiming its perceived historic territorial rights in the Pacific. How the United States addresses these emerging antiaccess threats while managing the growing competition with China for regional influence constitutes one of the critical defense policy issues of the coming decade. The answers will provide the basis on which the United States will be able to assist in maintaining the stability of the region or succeed in any future conflicts.

During the Cold War, Europe existed at the center of America's strategic focus. In the future, however, the Pacific Rim will likely replace Europe as a central feature of US geostrategy, accelerating the need for countering the antiaccess problem. Current US power-projection capabilities need improvement in order to meet future national security requirements within the region. All US military services have growing access issues that need to be addressed in a comprehensive, balanced approach within the next 10 to 15 years. This study seeks to address what the Air Force can do to answer this important issue.

This study investigates the following question: How can land-based airpower answer the emerging antiaccess challenge in the Pacific Rim? Specifically, it addresses the antiaccess challenge associated with the vulnerability of fixed theater bases and how to employ military forces from overseas bases in the Pacific Rim. Lastly, it offers a basing framework from which the United States can provide comprehensive coverage of the Pacific Rim to address any future conflict.

Countering antiaccess strategies in the Pacific Rim has important national implications for several reasons. First is the immense geopolitical impact. Increased US military force-projection capability within the region provides increased political flexibility and substantially increased coercive leverage and conveys a strengthened commitment between the United States and its Pacific Rim allies. Second, the use of airpower in addressing world crises on a wide spectrum from humanitarian relief to open conflict has continually grown over the last five decades and has the potential to continue its increase, on absolute and relative scales, in meeting US national security needs. Enhanced overseas basing options, which include airfields, create several important dynamics. They make a future adversary's antiaccess response more difficult because the United States has more options and locations. They decrease the vulnerability of US joint forces to military threats because an adversary faces multiple threats, each with unique and complementary capabilities. All military services are dependent upon fixed forward ports, airfields, and bases in-theater to conduct combat operations. With an expanded basing structure, an adversary cannot focus its defense efforts entirely upon denying a single US military force. Third, expanded basing would be entirely congruent with the Air Force's expeditionary air and space forces. Similarly, it provides a more substantial foundation for the Global Strike concept of operations (CONOPS), which focuses on countering emerging antiaccess forces.[2] All of these implications lead toward improved US and allied security within the Pacific Rim and the increased viability of joint and coalition forces.

In analyzing America's options for countering antiaccess threats, we must remember that this is not the first time the United States has faced a significant antiaccess threat. After World War II, the Soviet Union (USSR) emerged as a superpower rival. It presented the United States with multiple antiaccess difficulties, including a growing set of fixed-base vulnerabilities that the United States addressed quite aggressively throughout the Cold War, starting in the 1950s. Those challenges mirror in many ways the antiaccess threats facing the United States today in the Pacific Rim.

The development of Soviet atomic weapons and improved conventional military capabilities exposed the inherent vulnerabilities of overseas bases, especially in Europe. US Air Forces in Europe (USAFE), primarily fighters, and Strategic Air Command (SAC), primarily bombers and aerial refuelers, pursued multiple strategies to defeat the antiaccess challenges presented by Soviet nuclear weapons and conventional forces in Eastern Europe. In particular, USAFE developed dispersal plans for US tactical forces in Europe in case of Soviet atomic attack. In contrast, SAC decided to bring back their forward-deployed, long-range bombers from overseas and base them in continental United States (CONUS) locations. Yet, even SAC's strategy required increased dispersal and expanded forward basing. The increasing ranges of Soviet intercontinental ballistic missiles (ICBM) forced

SAC to develop dispersal plans within CONUS. Additionally, the development of new weapon systems in the 1950s, such as ICBMs, reflected the intense manner in which SAC fielded systems with a capability and employment strategy designed to defeat the Soviet antiaccess challenge. Because of the many interesting parallels they contain, the plans and weapon systems developed in the 1950s offer historical precedents that aid contemporary US defense policy in the Pacific Rim.

This study seeks to highlight this issue and stimulate debate by applying the lessons learned during the 1950s on how to increase survivability and decrease vulnerability of fixed land bases and weapon systems. These analogies will assist in providing multiple solutions to answer the growing antiaccess issue as adversaries increase their ability to exploit the vulnerability of aircraft on the ground and on aircraft carriers. Similarly, it will advocate basing and force-protection proposals designed to maintain offensive military advantages by shaping or defeating a potential adversary's strategy prior to execution. This discussion contributes to the development of a United States Air Force (USAF) basing framework in a plausible future antiaccess environment.

The research methodology used in this study involves historical and literature reviews, interviews, and a qualitative comparison of the current and emerging antiaccess problem in the Pacific Rim with US efforts in the 1950s and 1960s to counter the Soviet threat. Most of the evidence comes from primary-source documents declassified for this study. These documents are supplemented by secondary sources and interviews with defense analysts and military personnel. In terms of scope, this study attempts to provide broad, near-term (10–20 years) strategic- and operational-policy options.

Chapter 2 focuses on the current and emerging antiaccess threat in the Pacific Rim. Chapters 3 and 4 discuss in detail solutions developed by the United States in the 1950s to counter the Soviet Union's growing atomic threat. Chapter 3 explores the dispersal plans created by USAFE in the late 1950s as a partial answer to antiaccess problems posed by the Soviet Union. Chapter 4 traces the actions undertaken by SAC to protect its long-range bomber and tanker forces and the US development of the strategic triad that provided a more robust, balanced deterrent force. Chapter 5 builds on historic evidence, the Air Force's new Global Strike CONOPS, and currently proposed weapon systems acquisitions to supply an operational basing framework—a framework that is survivable, sustainable, agile, and mobile in a future high-threat environment. Finally, chapter 6 concludes with specific policy implications and areas for future study.

For a global power-projection nation like the United States, changing adversarial antiaccess strategies rather than facing some frightening new issue is actually a consistent historic dilemma that must be continuously reevaluated due to emerging technologies and new geopolitical realities. In the Pacific Rim, antiaccess challenges demand a comprehensive review of the future capabilities the USAF brings to the fight. The ability to effectively counter the emerging antiaccess problem in the Pacific Rim will enhance US's ability to project national power. This study offers a balanced, comprehensive approach, which strengthens the combat capability of all services in a joint environment. Its implications and proposals provide an admittedly limited view of an infinitely complicated issue. Yet, the question of how the USAF should best prepare to operate in an antiaccess environment is both politically and militarily consequential. The next chapter expands this discussion to focus on the nature and dynamics of that new—and in some ways, old—strategic environment.

Notes

1. Zalmay Khalilzad et al., *The United States and a Rising China*, RAND Report MR-1082-AF (Santa Monica, CA: RAND, 1999), 17.

2. Air Combat Command is the Air Force's lead agency on developing the Global Strike CONOPs. For a more detailed accounting of the Global Strike CONOPS, see Gen John P. Jumper, USAF, "Global Strike Task Force: A Transforming Concept, Forged by Experience," *Aerospace Power Journal* 15, no. 1 (Spring 2001): 24–33.

Chapter 2

The Antiaccess Challenge in the Pacific Rim

The Gulf War was a stunning victory. But it took six months of planning and transport to summon our fleets and divisions and position them for battle. In the future, we are unlikely to have that kind of time. Enemy ballistic and cruise missiles and weapons of mass destruction may make such operations difficult.

—Gov. George W. Bush
"A Period of Consequences," 1999

Projecting and sustaining U.S. forces in distant anti-access or area-denial environments and defeating anti-access and area-denial threats [is one of the OSD's critical operational goals].

—*Quadrennial Defense Review*, 2001

Antiaccess is a relatively new term that encompasses many of the age-old difficulties of projecting power into a distant region. Why has antiaccess become such a prevalent concern among defense analysts? This chapter addresses that question and suggests that countering antiaccess capabilities will be an increasingly dominant theme in debates over future force structure and thus should be a central concern for Air Force policy makers.

Antiaccess became an issue shortly after the end of the Cold War when defense visionary Andrew Marshall began to raise this concern with a succession of secretaries of defense in the 1990s.[1] In 1997 Congress commissioned the National Defense Panel (NDP)—a distinguished group of national strategy analysts and retired senior military officers—to provide a critical, independent review of the Pentagon's *Quadrennial Defense Review* (*QDR*).[2] In their report, which was substantially more aggressive than the Pentagon's, the NDP provided the initial framework of what constituted the antiaccess threat. The report stated:

> The cornerstone of America's continued military preeminence is our ability to project combat power rapidly and virtually unimpeded to widespread areas of the world. Much of our power projection capability depends on sustained access to regions of concern. Any number of circumstances might compromise our forward presence (both bases and forward operating forces) and therefore diminish our ability to apply military power, reducing our military and political influence in key regions of the world. For political (domestic or regional) reasons, allies might be coerced not to grant the United States access to their sovereign territory. . . .
>
> Even if we retain the necessary bases and port infrastructure to support forward deployed forces, they will be vulnerable to strikes that could reduce or neutralize their utility. Precision strikes, weapons of mass destruction, and cruise and ballistic missiles all present threats to our forward presence, particularly as stand-off ranges increase. . . .

At the same time, constraints on forward basing (i.e., infrastructure outside the continental United States: ports, installations, pre-positioned equipment, and airfields) and advanced technologies threaten to impede our access to key regions.[3]

The NDP report was quite influential in refocusing the defense debate on answering the antiaccess challenge and continues to resonate among national-level strategists, both civilian and military.

The antiaccess threat breaks down overlapping political, geographic, and military factors that could individually or collectively undermine US power projection capabilities in any future conflict.[4] Each antiaccess issue presents unique challenges. This study focuses on the Pacific Rim specifically for its emerging political prominence, difficult geography, and proliferation of developing military technologies. The Pacific Rim contains an unstable combination of declining and emerging regional powers, including China, India, Russia, Korea, Indonesia, Malaysia, and Japan. In particular, the possible emergence of China as an acquisitive regional hegemon must occupy any serious strategist's attention.[5] There are also several potential flash points that could erupt into open conflict at any time, such as Taiwan, Korea, and the Spratly Islands. Furthermore, the United States has traditionally faced varying degrees of difficulty in convincing reluctant allies to allow access during periods of crisis.

Any military operation in the Pacific Rim must transverse tremendous distances over water and often negotiate complex terrain. The overwater distances in the area are daunting when military operators consider operational requirements. Likewise, China and Russia possess substantial territorial landmasses which create considerable access difficulties for any potential operation. Lastly, dense vegetation is the prevalent foliage in the Pacific Rim. This has immense operational implications, especially when the vegetation complicates the targeting process.

Militarily, the list of current or emerging antiaccess technologies keeps growing and proliferating, creating dilemmas for all the services. Weapons of mass destruction continually pose a threat for military forces operating in-theater. Ground forces face ballistic missiles with submunitions, cruise missiles, and advanced aircraft—all enhanced by global positioning system (GPS) guidance. Maritime forces confront a dizzying array of mines, supersonic missiles, and quieter, longer-running diesel submarines. Air forces must cope with advanced "double-digit" surface-to-air missile systems in addition to threats against land bases. Space assets must defend against antisatellite capabilities, such as ground-based lasers or "dazzlers," that confuse satellite sensors. Additionally, commando forces and terrorist attacks constitute ongoing threats to US power-projection forces. Lastly, the increasing transparency of US military operations through the proliferation of commercial satellite imagery enhances an adversary's ability to target all deploying military forces more accurately. In 1999 a Defense Science Board (DSB) study on globalization and security proclaimed:

Access to commercial technology is virtually universal, and its exploitation for both civil and military ends is largely unconstrained. Many of the most important enabling technologies for information-intensive U.S. concepts of warfare (e.g., access to space, surveillance, sensors and signal processing, high fidelity simulation, and telecommunications) are equally available to the United States, our friends and allies, and potential U.S. adversaries.[6]

These antiaccess capabilities will continue to increase in the Pacific Rim, and with them, the threat to US power projection. Additionally, the US power-projection capability across the Pacific Rim is predominantly carrier-based. Overreliance on carriers creates a weakness, relying too heavily upon a single means of approach. A stronger US military access equation should involve a more balanced approach with air, land, and sea options. Collectively, three strong avenues of military access would enhance the security and effectiveness of each, and would thereby degrade an adversary's ability and willingness to counter US power projection. The Air Force, Navy, Army, and Marine Corps all have current and growing access issues which need to be addressed in a comprehensive, balanced approach within the next 10 to 15 years.

Land-based airpower is a critical component of any comprehensive joint plan to project power within the Pacific Rim. This study argues that the Air Force can provide significant, cost-effective contributions to US power-projection capability within the Pacific Rim.

Enhanced contributions by the Air Force will magnify four crucial components for future strategies. First, the overall joint effectiveness of US military forces will increase. The issue of addressing the antiaccess challenge is not entirely fixated upon the Air Force's overseas land bases. Instead, as the Air Force effectively answers the antiaccess challenge, the vulnerabilities of US joint forces will decrease. Similarly, all US forces are reliant on forward operating locations in order to execute military operations.[7] Second, an adversary will have a more difficult and complex challenge in addressing a more balanced US approach toward military power projection. Currently, US military power-projection capabilities are heavily weighted toward naval operations, which are also attempting to address the antiaccess challenge.[8] Balancing US power projection in the Pacific Rim will decelerate dedicated adversary efforts to deny US carrier battle groups, providing a powerful means of carrier protection. Third, military options available to US political leadership will increase. Increased options will provide the president an improved ability to creatively and selectively respond to dynamic regional crises. Fourth, enhanced capability directly increases credibility and reflects a stronger commitment toward US allies in the region. The question remains as to how land-based airpower can assume an increased strategic and operational role in answering the emerging antiaccess challenge in the Pacific Rim. This study will answer that question using the Air Force's existing air and space expeditionary force (AEF) while remaining within either currently funded or projected Air Force weapon systems acquisitions.

Lastly, this study complements and enhances the Air Force's Global Strike CONOPS, which addresses the military antiaccess issue of penetrating enemy air defenses and holding at risk adversary antiaccess forces that threaten the entire joint force.[9] This study focuses on the military antiaccess challenge associated with the vulnerability of fixed theater bases and how to employ military forces from overseas bases in the Pacific Rim. It accomplishes this by providing a basing framework from which the United States can provide comprehensive coverage of the Pacific Rim to answer any future conflict.

Adversaries Seeking Asymmetric Antiaccess Advantages

American aircraft at land bases represent a lucrative target for adversaries due to the dominant and growing role of airpower in US military operations. Historically, adversaries have attacked land bases as one aspect of an overall strategy for achieving air superiority.[10] Achieving air superiority allows attacks on an adversary's centers of gravity (COG) at will, while denying the opponent the ability to retaliate.[11] Airpower operates best when it is able to execute its missions relatively unmolested. Therefore, airfield protection is a vital concern to any US military campaign.

This fundamental principle of addressing or attacking base vulnerabilities was demonstrated during conflicts since World War I. US conflicts since 1990 (Operations Desert Storm, Deliberate Force, Allied Force, Enduring Freedom, and Iraqi Freedom) demonstrate a tremendous asymmetric advantage when the United States projects power to and from forward sanctuaries. Several factors contribute to this US asymmetric advantage. First, the collapse of the Soviet Union brought about the demise of the only adversary with a military force capable of inflicting significant damage upon US airfields worldwide. Second, successful conflicts since 1990 create an expectation pertaining to air operations that future theater commanders and political leaders will want to exploit.

Political and military leaders and the American public now expect successful execution of military operations anywhere in the world, at any time, with minimal risk to US military forces.[12] This is primarily due to US air dominance. Its success has bred a false sense of security, which future adversaries may well exploit. Many countries fully recognize the asymmetric advantages US airpower brings to any conflict. In the future, nations who view the United States as a potential adversary will likely focus their efforts on denying the United States the ability to operate its aircraft from unopposed airfields within the region. Therefore, it would be a significant mistake to believe that the uncontested projection of power by US forces will continue into the future. Future adversaries will adapt their methods to deny, prevent, or delay the unopposed buildup of US forces in distant regions.[13]

Accordingly, an adaptive adversary will attempt to employ its strengths versus perceived US weaknesses. The NDP identified several courses of action a future adversary may initiate to undermine US power-projection efforts. These include attacking the will to fight; employing imaginative tactics and techniques; denying access to forward locations; exploiting WMD technologies; targeting fixed installations and massed formations; moving the fight to urban areas; and combining approaches for even greater synergy.[14] These approaches represent the antiaccess challenges military strategists must take into account as they attempt to nullify future threats.

Echoing and amplifying the 1997 NDP report, the Department of Defense's (DOD) 2001 *QDR* concluded that the antiaccess challenge is one of the most significant strategic threats facing future US power-projection operations.[15] The *QDR* report states that "projecting and sustaining US forces in distant antiaccess or area-denial environments and defeating antiaccess and area-denial threats" is one of six key operational goals driving the need for transformation.[16] Specifically aimed at the Pacific Rim, the report states,

> Asia is gradually emerging as a region susceptible to large-scale military competition. Along a broad arc of instability that stretches from the Middle East to Northeast Asia, the region contains a volatile mix of rising and declining regional powers. . . . Many of these states field large militaries and possess the potential to develop or acquire weapons of mass destruction. . . .
>
> The possibility exists that a military competitor with a formidable resource base will emerge in the region.[17]

Similarly, a 1999 DSB study on globalization and security highlighted, once again, the ability of nations to rather cost-effectively and asymmetrically develop antiaccess capabilities designed to deter or deny US power-projection capabilities. The study estimated that

> potential U.S. regional adversaries spending on the order of only $15–20 billion over a decade in the global marketplace could develop robust theater-denial/disruption capabilities. These include conventional anti-naval forces (e.g., ultra-quiet diesel submarines, advanced anti-ship cruise missiles, and sophisticated sea mines); theater-range ballistic and land-attack cruise missiles (with the latter expected to be available in the thousands, and, increasingly, with low-observable characteristics); and nuclear, chemical, and biological weapons.[18]

China represents a clear example of a nation developing significant antiaccess capabilities. Although the future dynamics of the relationship between the United States and China cannot be predicted, China's emerging military capabilities, combined with its geographic size and location, pose a difficult challenge. Therefore, this study will use China in the Pacific Rim as an example of the antiaccess and basing challenges the United States faces in the near future. The reader should keep in mind that many nations and combinations of nations could also develop substantial antiaccess capabilities as well. China is representative of the general threat.

China will likely target current US basing vulnerability through a robust antiaccess strategy which will entail geopolitical and threat-based means. It will employ an antiaccess strategy built on the simple fact that US forces will have to overcome time, distance, and third-party constraints (e.g.,

11

China will attempt to coerce Japan, Korea, the Philippines, and Thailand) in order to influence events in the Pacific Rim. First, China will attempt to geopolitically isolate the United States through diplomacy. It will attempt to portray in international media outlets that the United States is inappropriately involved in regional affairs that should not concern it. Furthermore, China will denounce US actions as destabilizing to the region. By doing this it will seek to influence nations, such as Japan and Korea (nations with major US installations) and Thailand and the Philippines (nations that could immediately support US operations), from allowing US operations from their homelands. If successful, China will hamstring US power projection and force the United States to overcome substantial geographic and military obstacles with reduced forces. Similarly, the compelling value of US military superiority might be diminished by a Chinese belief that various political constraints will inhibit the United States' will to use it (e.g., the Chinese perception that US sensitivity to casualties will limit its military actions).[19] Second, if required, China will attempt to implement its emerging threat-based antiaccess capabilities against the United States and any regional supporting allies or potential coalition partners. China's combination of ballistic, subsonic cruise, and supersonic Sunburn/Moskit cruise missiles provides a significant antiaccess capability.[20] These capabilities raise the costs for the United States in supporting allies in the Pacific Rim. Although overall US military power vastly exceeds that of China, the Chinese might believe that a surprise attack by a large number of missiles could inflict serious damage on US power-projection capabilities, thereby producing a serious psychological shock or deterrent threat that would hamper further US action.

As the United States develops a comprehensive strategy for enabling power projection into the Pacific Rim, it must protect its perceived weaknesses. In the future, an adversary will look to favor asymmetric advantages by exploiting US vulnerabilities. The DOD ascertained that potential future adversaries could attempt to use surprise and deception as part of antiaccess strategies.[21] The execution of these strategies will be enhanced by the potential use of WMDs and precision conventional weapons, which may include ballistic and cruise missiles, antiship missiles, sea mines, and diesel submarines.[22]

By implementing this strategy, an adversary can hope to minimize US coercive power. In their article, "Defeating US Coercion," Daniel Byman and Matthew Waxman present five elements of US coercion that China may attempt to exploit. These elements include: (1) a preference for multilateralism, (2) intolerance for American casualties, (3) aversion to enemy civilian suffering, (4) reliance on high-technology options, and (5) commitment to international norms.[23] Subsequently, to counter potential adversarial coercive attempts in the Pacific Rim, the United States must ensure that it retains and enhances its ties with various key nations in the region, employ means that minimize American and civilian casualties, share risks instead of withdrawing to the CONUS, escalate the perception of US stakes, reinforce the credibility of its actions, and enhance its perceived commitment towards the region through participation and leadership in multinational institutions like the United Nations.[24] Therefore, the United States has begun the processes of looking at options for countering antiaccess strategies and defending base vulnerabilities.

Following the 1997 NDP report, the *QDR* report stated, "The cornerstone of America's continued military preeminence is our ability to project combat power rapidly and virtually unimpeded to widespread areas of the globe."[25] Currently, power-projection strategies depend on US forces having sufficient time to build up in-theater as well as gaining rapid access to theater bases, ports, airfields, and littoral waters. However, the United States cannot expect future adversaries to allow its military forces to exploit time and space to their sole advantage.[26] Potential adversaries recognize and are actively preparing to exploit this vulnerability.[27] Thus, the NDP report states that, "adaptive enemies, emerging technologies, greater distances, and altered alliance relations will present new conditions to US military forces that must be mastered if we are to maintain our current capability to project power."[28] In response to these national-level reviews on the future security environment, significant military planning efforts are under way to understand the antiaccess challenge and develop effective counterstrategies.

One such effort is the Air Force's dedicated antiaccess concept, the Global Strike CONOPS, its attempt to link together the capabilities of future weapon systems procurement, CONOPS, organizational constructs, and doctrine to most effectively answer the antiaccess challenge. Since the Gulf War, the Air Force has undergone significant transformation from a Cold War–legacy force to an expeditionary force that combines new technologies, new organizational constructs, new CONOPS, and doctrine to retain and expand America's asymmetric advantage—air and space power. The Global Strike CONOPS was developed to provide robust access capabilities into a theater, to ensure survivability of those capabilities at fixed locations, and to sustain assets in-theater.[29]

Fortunately, leaders whose formative maturation experiences occurred in the 1970s and 1980s currently command the Air Force. They share a common understanding that military forces must prepare to conduct operations from within threat rings under severe antiaccess conditions. For them the Soviet Union was a very real and dangerous threat. However, this reveals a follow-on concern. The new generation that was raised on the Gulf War and beyond has only operated in a permissive environment and will not be as focused on or as amenable to engaging the emerging antiaccess challenge. In many ways, the new generation grew up in the halcyon days of airpower.

The Soviet Union, from the 1950s until the end of the Cold War, presented the United States with the most deadly antiaccess capabilities ever created. The threat of massive Soviet conventional military forces pouring through the Fulda Gap or nuclear missiles raining down upon our forces

13

and airfields, both overseas and in the CONUS, was a mammoth concern. Tremendous efforts went into continuously planning, training, and equipping to fight against this potential onslaught. US military forces prepared to operate under the most cataclysmic conditions imaginable, whether nuclear, chemical, or biological. The decision was made to overcome these hazardous operational conditions through innovative operational concepts, technological advancements, and organizational adaptations.

Air Force actions in the 1950s in response to the burgeoning Soviet nuclear and conventional military capabilities provide ample lessons for the future conduct of military operations in the Pacific Rim. The following two chapters will discuss efforts by USAFE and SAC, respectively, in response to that Cold War threat.

Notes

1. Andrew Marshall (School of Advanced Air and Space Studies), interview by the author, 4 December 2002.

2. Christopher J. Bowie, *The Anti-Access Threat and Theater Air Bases* (Washington, DC: Center for Strategic and Budgetary Assessments, 2002), 1; and NDP, *Report of the National Defense Panel on Transforming Defense: National Security in the 21st Century* (Arlington, VA: National Defense Panel, December 1997). The distinguished panel members include Philip Odeen; Hon. Richard Armitage; Gen Richard D. Hearney, USMC, retired; Adm David E. Jeremiah, USN, retired; Hon. Robert M. Kimmitt; Dr. Andrew F. Krepinevich; Gen James McCarthy, USAF, retired; Dr. Janne E. Nolan; and Gen Robert W. RisCassi, USA, retired.

3. NDP, *Report on Transforming Defense*, 12–13.

4. The framework for thinking about antiaccess in terms of political, geographic, and military issues comes from the excellent work at the Northrup-Grumman Analysis Center by Christopher Bowie and Robert Haffa. Bowie, *Anti-Access Threat*, 1.

5. For in-depth analysis regarding the potential of China emerging as a regional hegemon, read Aaron L. Friedberg, "The Struggle for Mastery in Asia," *Commentary* 110, no. 4 (November 2000): 17–27; and Khalilzad et al., *The United States and a Rising China*.

6. DSB, *Final Report of the Defense Science Board Task Force on Globalization and Security* (Washington, DC: Office of the Undersecretary of Defense for Acquisition and Technology, December 1999), 21–22.

7. Bowie, *Anti-Access Threat*, 4.

8. For a more complete picture of the Navy's efforts in solving potential antiaccess challenges, see Owen R. Coté Jr., *Assuring Access and Projecting Power: The Navy in the New Security Environment* (Cambridge, MA: MIT Security Studies Program, 2001).

9. For a more complete picture of Global Strike CONOPS, read Jumper, "Global Strike Task Force," 24–33. A quick synopsis of the Global Strike CONOPS can be found at http://www.globalsecurity.org/military/agency/usaf/gstf.htm (accessed 14 November 2006).

10. Aviation pioneer Giulio Douhet first stated in print the importance of airfields for gaining command of the air. He stated, "Similarly, destroying an enemy's airplanes by seeking them out in the air is, while not entirely useless, the least effective method. A much better way is to destroy his airports, bases, and centers of production. In the air his planes may escape; but, like the birds whose nests and eggs have been destroyed, those planes which were still out would have no bases at which to alight when they returned." Giulio Douhet, *The Command of the Air* (Salem, NH: Ayers Company Publishers, Inc., 1984), 30.

11. Carl von Clausewitz coined the original usage of centers of gravity in his seminal work, *On War*. This study uses Col John A. Warden's concept of COGs. See Col John A. Warden III, "The Enemy as a System," *Airpower Journal* 9, no. 1 (Spring 1995): 40–55.

12. John Stillion and David T. Orletsky write, "These operations were conducted against an adversary who lacked the means, will, skill, and vision to attempt to attack and disrupt USAF aircraft and operations where they are most vulnerable—at their fixed operating bases." John Stillion and David T. Orletsky, *Airbase Vulnerability to Conventional Cruise-Missile and Ballistic-Missile Attacks: Technoogy, Scenarios, and U.S. Air Force Responses*, RAND Report MR-1028-AF (Santa Monica, CA: RAND, 1999), 2. Furthermore, the authors attempt to address why Iraq failed to strike at the coalition base vulnerability during the Gulf War. The three main reasons were: the coalition air defenses were too powerful; Iraqi ballistic missiles (SCUD) were not accurate enough; and Iraq was unable or unwilling to organize special operations forces attacks against airfields (ibid., 6).

13. Ibid., 11.

14. Ibid.

15. Bowie, *Anti-Access Threat*, 1.

16. Donald Rumsfeld, *Quadrennial Defense Review* (Washington, DC: Office of the Secretary of Defense, 30 September 2001), 30.

17. Ibid., 4.

18. DSB, *Final Report of the Defense Science Board*, 25.

19. For a richer discussion of the complex relationship between the United States and China in the international arena, see Abram N. Shulsky, *Deterrence Theory and Chinese Behavior*, RAND Report MR-1161-AF (Santa Monica, CA: RAND, 2000); and Michael Pillsbury, *China Debates the Future Security Environment* (Washington, DC: National Defense University Press, 2000).

20. For more complete information on China's missile capabilities, see Frank W. Moore, "China's Military Capabilities," *Institute for Defense and Disarmament Studies*, Policy Studies no. 2, June 2000, http://www.comw.org/cmp/fulltext/iddschina.html (accessed 15 November 2006).

21. Rumsfeld, *QDR*, 2001, III–IV.

22. Gen Richard E. Hawley, Michael B. Donley, and John R. Backschies, "Enhancing USAF's Pacific Posture," *Armed Forces Journal International* 140, no. 2 (September 2002): 54–56.

23. Daniel Byman and Matthew Waxman, "Defeating US Coercion," *Survival* 41, no. 2 (Summer 1999): 107–20.

24. Joseph S. Nye Jr. advocates aggressively for the United States to use multilateralist approaches to foreign policy. For a greater depth in understanding this approach, read Joseph Nye, *The Paradox of American Power: Why the World's Only Superpower Can't Go it Alone* (New York: Oxford University Press, 2002).

25. NDP, *Report on Transforming Defense*, 12.

26. USAF Quadrennial Defense Review, *Joint Freedom of Action: Defeating Anti-Access Strategies*, USAF White Paper (Washington, DC: USAF, May 2001), 1.

27. The 1999 DSB study on globalization and security added, "Those states preparing for potential conflict with the United States will seek to capitalize on the great distances U.S. forces must travel to engage them, and on U.S. forces' near-absolute reliance on unimpeded access to and use of ports, airfields, bases, and littoral waters in the theater of conflict." DSB, *Final Report of the Defense Science Board*, 25.

28. NDP, *Report on Transforming Defense*, 13.

29. The Global Strike CONOPS was born in a 2001 Air Force QDR Office initiative called the global reconnaissance strike (GRS) concept, which linked stealthy, long-range joint forces in a dedicated antiaccess effort. GRS became the basis for many of the recommendations in the subsequent QDR report and was the genesis of today's Global Strike CONOPS. Col Tom Ehrhard, interview by author, 22 April 2003.

Chapter 3

USAFE's Dispersed
Journey—Back to the Future

The period which we all realized must some day come when intercontinental air warfare would be a possibility is now at hand. . . . Air Force thought and action is oriented about the concept that our primary effort must be directed towards providing the means of surviving such an atomic phase, not only without disaster, but so that our relative strength would be such that we may mobilize and bring to bear any forces that may be required to assure victory.

—Gen Muir S. Fairchild, 7 February 1950

On 23 September 1950, Pres. Harry S. Truman stated, "We have evidence that within recent weeks an atomic explosion occurred in the USSR."[1] With these simple words, Truman notified the American people that the Soviets now possessed atomic weapons. The immediate ramifications were not lost upon American officials, who were "shaken by the knowledge that the Soviets had the A-bomb."[2] The perception of eventual US vulnerability to a Soviet atomic weapons attack, both at home and abroad, skyrocketed. The US belief that it enjoyed a significant technological advantage over the Soviets evaporated with a single atomic blast. The emergence of the Cold War exposed US and USSR tensions as a cataclysmic struggle between superpowers for world influence.

This section focuses on several actions taken by both the US Air Forces in Europe and the Strategic Air Command (covered in the next chapter), as they addressed how to survive and operate under the enormous threat of Soviet atomic weapons strikes and massive Soviet conventional military forces.

The Soviets viewed the development of ICBMs and intermediate-range ballistic missiles (IRBM) as the mechanism for eliminating several distinct disadvantages and creating new leverages against the United States. First, ICBMs would bridge the technological gap in delivery systems for atomic weapons between the Soviets and the Americans. Second, ICBMs would provide the predominant force for the Soviets to counterbalance the US strategic bomber advantage. Third, a fully developed ICBM and IRBM force supplied the Soviets with the capability to carry out coercive strategies against the United States. In other words, ballistic missiles allowed the Soviets the potential to strike the United States and its allies anywhere in the world with atomic weapons. There would be no more safe havens—US soil would lie within atomic threat rings. Therefore, the Soviets poured their resources into developing enormous rockets with the capability to carry heavy yields of nuclear weapons anywhere in the world.[3] These events triggered massive changes in force structure and operations in the US political and military communities.

Likewise in the Pacific Rim today, the United States faces a rising antiaccess threat of not only nuclear weapons but precision-equipped, conventionally armed ballistic and cruise missiles. China is investing heavily in military technology capable of denying the United States access into the region. US reactions to the Soviet Union's acquisition of long-range weapons in the 1950s can aid in our approach to managing rising antiaccess threats today.

The entry of the USSR into the "atomic club," along with several other contextual factors, ripped open congressional purse strings.[4] Specifically, the Soviet atomic blast and the commencement of the Korean War, followed by revelations of successful Soviet ICBM launches, expedited a fourfold increase in the defense budget.[5] A bipolar world order quickly developed, which would become dominated politically and militarily by growing and increasingly capable nuclear arsenals.[6] These arsenals were designed to compel and deter US actions, and if all else failed, to annihilate the United States. Western Europe became the focal point for the immense East-West struggle for dominance. US allegiance to the North Atlantic Treaty Organization (NATO), formed in April 1949, required the forward basing of significant amounts of US military forces to act as a counterweight to expanding Soviet and Eastern Bloc military forces.[7]

During the early to mid-1950s, the survivability and operability of airpower in Europe was pivotal in deterring and countering potential Soviet acts of aggression. As the strongest airpower arm in NATO, USAFE provided the backbone of military forces capable of retaliating against the Soviets. USAFE assets offered NATO two crucial coercion strategy elements: deterrence and compellence.[8] First, USAFE and all US forces stationed in Europe delivered an important message to the Soviets about the US commitment to defending the "free world" from any further Soviet expansionistic desires. A strong show of US military force signaled to the Soviets the willingness of the United States to counter any threats. Second, these forward-deployed military assets provided a compellent capability, which could either convey an increasing US resolve or physically punish aggressive acts. During the 1950s, the United States believed the Soviets possessed the will to initiate an atomic attack. Thus, USAFE's ability to conduct combat operations against the Soviet threat required the capacity to survive initial and succeeding atomic attacks and to retaliate in the face of such attacks.[9] Similarly, this analysis suggests that the United States must continue to develop operational concepts designed to answer the growing antiaccess challenge in the Pacific Rim. In order to mass persistent, overwhelming firepower, the United States requires land-based airpower operating within known threat rings. As in the 1950s, these land bases need the capability to survive an initial attack and then achieve and maintain a sustainable level of operations.

USAFE installations were perceived to be the prime targets for any Soviet atomic campaign because the major part of the atomic retaliatory capability of NATO was concentrated in USAFE units. As of 1 December 1954, USAFE based its combat air forces in the United Kingdom and central Europe at a total of 15 airfields. Similarly, USAFE established its logistic support capabilities at two major depots at Burtonwood in England and Chateauroux in France.[10] Based on the vulnerability of limited USAFE force and logistics locations and the Soviet atomic threat, a warning proclaimed that "as few as 15 well-placed atomic weapons could constitute a fatal blow."[11] The perception existed among senior US and NATO leadership that a Soviet atomic first strike would eradicate USAFE. This motivated NATO and specifically the USAF to develop survival methods for its air forces. In response, USAFE developed detailed dispersal plans as a means of increasing the survivability of its combat resources. These dispersal plans are relevant for future operational concepts designed to answer the antiaccess challenge in the Pacific Rim.

The purpose of the USAFE dispersal program was "to provide sufficient dispersal to reduce to a minimum those factors contributing to a major target or area for atomic attack while still retaining an operational sortie capability."[12] Additionally, the USAFE commander in chief (CINCUSAFE), Lt Gen William H. Tunner, stated that the operational concept of dispersed operations was "vital to the ability of USAFE to counter the Soviet air threat in this atomic age." General Tunner designated the development of dispersed operations as a "must" program and a command project of the highest priority that needed to be achieved at minimum cost in resources.[13]

The central fighting unit of USAFE was a combat wing or main operating base (MOB). USAFE used conventional air base patterns to design and build its tactical air bases in Europe. Normally, these bases provided for the operation and maintenance of a full wing or more of aircraft.[14] Each wing became further divided into separate squadron areas, which often used dispersed hardstands for housing aircraft. Hardstands were metal walls which shielded the aircraft on two sides and offered some blast protection. These measures provided a greater degree of force protection from conventional air attack. Yet, due to the concentration of forces at one location, the use of dispersal hardstands would not prevent the destruction of an entire wing by a single atomic bomb.[15]

Dispersed Aircraft Operations

An operational solution was needed. The command instituted a USAFE dispersal program that required combat wings to disperse into geographically separated squadron-sized units, or "squadron complex systems," in times of rising tensions between NATO and the Soviet Union. When a combat wing or MOB dispersed, each squadron complex system deployed to a separate airfield. The squadron complex systems remained networked to the main operating base for logistical and command requirements. Optimally, the desired minimal separation between the individually deployed squadron airfields was approximately 30 miles. Theoretically, this separation would provide the protection needed for several squadron complexes to survive an atomic attack.[16]

Under the USAFE dispersal program, each squadron complex consisted of one dispersed operating base (DOB), one dispersed landing area (DLA), and one dispersed parking area (DPA).[17] Furthermore, within a squadron complex system, the dispersed bases—DOBs and DLAs—required a separation of approximately 10 miles. Under the squadron complex system, the DOB functioned as the primary operating base for the squadron, and the DLA served as a secondary operational base. To provide protection against "moderate yield atomic weapons," the DPAs were to be located approximately three miles from one of the dispersed bases. Specially designed trailers towed aircraft between the parking area and the airfield. According to design requirements, facilities were intentionally constructed to minimum standards and were sufficient only to support combat operations on a wartime basis.[18] In concert, the squadron complex system improved the force protection of USAFE aircraft by providing greater survivability through dispersion, increasing targeting difficulties for a potential adversary, and signaling to allies and enemies a willingness to operate under extremely adverse conditions.

Headquarters USAFE prepared most of the dispersal program in early 1954, just as Soviet ballistic missile programs were thought to be maturing. The dispersal objective for planners was to provide sufficient DOBs to allow every squadron from each existing combat wing to conduct separated operations. Furthermore, each squadron and combat wing required a separate DLA for an even higher degree of dispersal. Lastly, each MOB or DOB required either a DLA, a DPA, or a combination of both.[19]

Squadrons could either operate from the MOBs, DOBs, or DLAs, depending on the requirements of the combat environment. These locations operated on a tiered concept of logistical support, with more services available at the MOBs. Servicing and munitions loading of aircraft could occur at all dispersed locations except for the DPAs. Mechanically, the MOBs performed major maintenance, while the dispersed locations accomplished any minor maintenance that their mobile equipment could handle. Subsequently, the DPAs were to serve as concealment locations to deny enemy reconnaissance from detecting their positions.[20] The DPAs provided additional force protection through dispersal and concealment of war-fighting assets.

Passive Defenses

Physical dispersal represented a pillar of USAFE's reaction to the rising nuclear threat, but its plan also contained specific passive defense measures. The passive defense portion of the USAFE dispersal program provided for the protection of aircraft and equipment by a myriad of means, including shelters and revetments, local early warning systems, the toning down of colors at key installations, concealment and local dispersal of offensive force components, deception devices, installation security measures, stockpiles of selected supplies, and standby equipment.[21] Several key aspects emerged from these passive measures. First, USAFE planners believed that casualties from all types of enemy attacks might be greatly reduced by using shelters. They also believed that the revetments would reduce the vulnerability of aircraft, vehicles, and maintenance and medical facilities. Second, they emphasized the use of local dispersal, concealment, and deception as a significant aspect of protecting crucial resources. They recognized that many simple cost-effective measures could potentially enhance the survivability of combat assets.

Third, planners accounted for the increased need for support equipment. Several pieces of equipment stood out in importance. Notably, planners wanted more air-transportable emergency refueling units, which consisted of one or more hydrant refueling subunits for rapid refueling of aircraft under emergency conditions. Potentially, each subunit could refuel six aircraft simultaneously. Furthermore, the DLAs' refueling tank trunks or the DOBs' underground storage tanks could resupply the mobile subunits' storage tanks. This flexible system provided for the quick emergency refueling of aircraft at USAFE MOBs in the event of any damage to normal refueling systems. It also provided a mobile system for use on DOBs and DLAs. Also of note, planners included standby materials and equipment for repairing potential bomb damage, especially to runways, taxiways, and hardstands. Planners allocated materials and equipment sufficient to repair bomb damage to sustain operations during the first 90 days of enemy air attacks. These materials and equipment were to be prepositioned on or near the installations, easily accessible in times of emergency. In conjunction, each combat wing's engineer aviation unit organized a mobile repair team to conduct these time-critical operations.[22]

Implementing the USAFE Dispersal Program

Although the dispersal plan appeared operationally sound, it would require both higher headquarters and political approval due to the increased costs associated with the concept. On 24 May 1954, a USAFE headquarters team presented the USAFE dispersal program draft proposal to Twelfth Air Force and four days later to the office of the air deputy of Supreme Headquarters Allied Powers Europe (SHAPE).[23] Twelfth Air Force commander, Maj Gen Robert M. Lee, accepted the USAFE proposal as the basis for study and expressed a desire to add a major rear-area logistics center to the plan. Additionally, Twelfth Air Force staff emphasized the importance of providing greater detail in the augmentation schedule, command and control, concept of operations, and communications network.[24] Overall, Twelfth Air Force was receptive to the initial plan and began preparations to develop the basing network and detailed operational considerations.

Subsequently at SHAPE, the USAFE briefing team conferred with Brig Gen Henry Vicellio, chief of Operations, and Brig Gen Harold C. Donnelly, chief of the Plans, Policy, and Operations Division. Both generals highlighted two key considerations: the increased requirement for additional airlift to support the dispersal plan and the high costs of any new construction. Despite those challenges, the USAFE team stressed the desirability of accepting forward dispersal due to the looming Soviet threat. General Donnelly immediately stated that forward dispersal was necessary for survival and that Air Chief Marshall Sir Basil Embry, Royal Air Force, Allied Air Forces Central Europe (AAFCE) commander, shared this belief.[25] In sum, SHAPE agreed with the USAFE dispersal program in principle. In support of this program, they named Col Joseph E. Gill of the SHAPE Logistics Division to lead a team of USAFE and NATO personnel to Washington in mid-June 1954 to present the dispersal problem to the Department of the Air Force.[26]

The combined SHAPE/USAFE briefing team's presentations were well received in Washington. All staff sections visited by the group were receptive to the dispersal and passive-defense ideas, and all were interested in the USAFE dispersal program concept. Similar to the presentations' reception at SHAPE, the Office of the Deputy Chief of Staff for Operations of the Department of the Air Force approved of the dispersal in principle. Additionally, the key officers of the Department of the Air Force viewed the proposed USAFE dispersal concept as a part of a worldwide Air Force problem.[27]

Acting upon this view, on 9 July 1954, Air Force vice chief of staff Gen Thomas D. White informed the USAFE commander in chief that he was directing the Air University commander to establish a project to develop methods for reducing the vulnerability of tactical air forces on the ground, thus sustaining their operational capability to fulfill their combat missions. General White considered this avenue the best and quickest way to solve the problem. He directed that General Tunner provide supplemental support for the project.[28]

At the same time, General Tunner and Air Marshal Embry formed a team between USAFE headquarters and AAFCE headquarters on the dispersal project. Air Marshal Embry fully supported the USAFE dispersal program and promised his cooperation.[29]

Further Development of the USAFE Dispersal Program

Meanwhile, back at USAFE, further actions were undertaken to continue the rapid development of dispersal operations. On 17 June 1954, Brig Gen Royden E. Beebe, assistant chief of staff for Operations, requested the USAFE assistant chiefs of staff for Personnel, Intelligence, Material, Communications, and Installations appoint officers from their sections to form a working group, chaired by Col M. E. Marston of the Operations Plans Division.[30] The working group's objective would be to provide an overall directive to Headquarters Twelfth Air Force for further development of dispersal plans. The directive would require that Twelfth Air Force specifically address the following requirements:

1. A recommendation for the extent of implementation in peace-time.
2. The operational system to be followed, including the types of units and aircraft.
3. Command and intelligence systems.
4. Supply systems and pre-positioning locations.
5. Maintenance specifications, equipment, and locations.
6. Communications systems, equipment, and locations.
7. Depot relationships.
8. Air and surface transportation requirements and networks.
9. Installation specifications.[31]

By the end of July, the broad framework of the dispersal plan that USAFE requested Twelfth Air Force to prepare was firm. The fundamental concept remained the dispersal of a combat wing (MOB) into a squadron complex system (DOB, DLA, and DPA). Much of the original USAFE dispersal program remained. First, the dispersed locations' facilities were to be built in accordance with absolute minimum construction standards, sufficient only for the support of combat operations. Second, the plan required the maximum use of mobile and portable equipment for communications, maintenance, and supply activities. Third, peacetime flying operations would use existing combat wings on a full-time basis. Furthermore, the continual use of training alerts would exercise the dispersed locations. Based on supporting this dispersal rotation concept, USAFE predicted that possibly one-quarter to one-third of Twelfth Air Force would be deployed at any given time. The rotational element would allow all tactical squadrons to participate periodically, up to three or four times a year. Conditions at deployed locations entailed living in tents under field conditions and eating field or emergency rations. The development of the dispersal plans, at least on paper, was moving forward rapidly. General Tunner stated, "The operational pattern which will arise from a dispersed posture will be new and a departure from current operational concepts. We must test dispersal under circumstances designed to provide maximum assurance of workability, in order to develop wing and squadron operational problems and try to solve them before we are forced into this type operation by enemy action."[32]

On 28 August 1954 Twelfth Air Force commenced four tasks related to the dispersal program: (1) selecting 17 sites from a list proposed by USAFE for development to improve dispersal capabilities; (2) aligning the sites selected with squadron complex system requirements issued in prior USAFE studies on dispersal operations; (3) reviewing tentative standards for DOBs and DLAs as previously provided by USAFE; and (4) selecting potential autobahn landing strips.[33] USAFE and Twelfth Air Force staffs recognized early the operational flexibility to be gained by constructing all 17 sites.[34]

The proposed combat wings selected for subsequent development of the dispersed complex system included Bitburg, Hahn, Landstuhl, Spangdahlem, and Sembach—all in West Germany. Each of these MOBs would be provided one or two DOBs, two DLAs, and at least two DPAs.[35]

On 29 December 1954, General Tunner and his staff met with Brig Gen M. Gross, deputy commander of the Twelfth Air Force, and members of his staff. Specifically, this meeting addressed the types and amounts of maintenance accomplished at the various types of dispersal sites: MOBs, DOBs, DLAs, DPAs, and rear-echelon maintenance consolidated operational centers. Additionally, manpower requirements for the implementation of the USAFE dispersal program were discussed.[36]

General Tunner concluded the meeting by summarizing the USAFE dispersal decisions up to that time. First, squadron maintenance needed to occur at the DOBs. Aircraft of each dispersed tactical squadron would exercise at the DLAs and DPAs. Second, frequent usage of dispersed locations would occur either during planned exercises or if increased international tension required. Except for these occurrences, only minimal personnel would occupy them. Third, maintenance and supply elements would deploy to the rear-echelon maintenance consolidated operational sites concurrently with tactical squadrons at dispersed locations. Fourth, field maintenance and engine buildup would occur in rear areas. Large, transport-type aircraft would move supplies to dispersed operational locations.[37]

Protection of USAFE Dispersal Bases

USAFE recognized that the dispersal sites needed to be properly defended. Therefore, in early August 1954, USAFE requested the assistance of US Army Europe (USAREUR) in obtaining 50 mm antiaircraft guns. USAFE believed the 50 mm guns were soon to be surplus equipment because of the programmed conversion of the 32nd Antiaircraft Artillery (AAA) Brigade in the United Kingdom to the radar-guided 75 mm Skysweeper AAA system. USAFE intended to use these surplus guns for the defense of dispersed air bases.[38] To justify its request, USAFE prepared a study for the US commander in chief Europe (USCINCEUR). The study estimated that 300 of the 50 mm guns were releasable due to the conversion. USAFE's primary plan was to employ them against enemy low-level bombing and strafing attacks and to support local ground defense efforts.[39] The reallocation of the 50 mm antiaircraft guns to USAFE dispersed locations would directly support USAFE's dispersal concept.

Ultimately, USCINCEUR regarded the 50 mm multiple-mount antiaircraft guns as highly desirable weapons. Therefore, while offering no immediate resolution, USCINCEUR promised to keep USAFE requirements for AAA in mind when drafting new air defense plans.[40] Although USAFE was initially unable to receive AAA equipment to defend dispersed locations, the effort reflected its consideration and desire to accomplish base defense operations.

Acquisition of Tactical Aircraft Dispersal Trailers

As previously mentioned, USAFE's dispersal concept required the movement of planes from DOBs and DLAs to DPAs. Gen Lauris Norstad, the SHAPE air deputy, recommended development of an efficient way to transport aircraft between dispersed locations. Consequently, two tactical aircraft trailers, Type I and Type II, were designed.[41] Type I was a multiple-wheel model, and Type II was a tracklaying model. Both could transport all the types of tactical aircraft used in USAFE in either day or night operations. Five-ton trucks or tractors could pull the trailers loaded with aircraft. Additionally, the aircraft could be loaded onto the trailers within 10 minutes.[42]

In December 1954 the trailers were successfully tested at Wiesbaden AB, Germany. The test required towing aircraft with a load capacity of 30,000 pounds over rough terrain. Based on test results, USAFE selected the Type I model and, on 10 December 1954, placed an order for 115 Type I trailers.[43] The development of trailers that could quickly and safely transport airplanes across moderate terrain offered additional local airfield dispersal options.

Exercising the Dispersal Plan—Operation Vapor Trail

USAFE wanted to expedite the dispersal program because they feared the pace of Soviet IRBM development. Yet, before construction of dispersed locations could begin, USAFE was required to conduct an operational exercise, Vapor Trail, to prove the plausibility of successfully accomplishing dispersed operations. The results of Exercise Vapor Trail and the future of the dispersal program were interlinked.[44] However, the Twelfth Air Force dispersal plan enabled USAFE to proceed with final planning for the entire dispersal program while awaiting results of the exercise. Furthermore, USAFE continued to task the Twelfth Air Force with resolving additional planning considerations. Six elements of the dispersal plan required further development: the extent of maintenance to be accomplished at the DOB; materiel requirements for each type of installation; command organization lines within and between the wings and the rear-echelon maintenance consolidated operations; the minimum essential manpower augmentation necessary for the planned dispersal; the number of caretaker personnel to be permanently retained at the DOBs and DLAs; and realistic cost data.[45] Similarly, any future dispersed operational concept needed to address maintenance and personnel issues, particularly as they apply to footprint size.

USAFE's purpose in conducting Exercise Vapor Trail was to test the feasibility of the dispersed concept of operations outlined in the USAFE dispersal program. The program aimed at reducing the vulnerability of USAFE to possible enemy attack through dispersed operations. The primary concept for reduction of vulnerability of land bases from atomic attack rested upon split-wing operations. Combat wings deployed their flying squadrons to dispersed bases in the forward area, and a rear-echelon support base would perform major maintenance and supply aircraft parts. The main objective of Exercise Vapor Trail was to determine how USAFE units could sustain an acceptable degree of operational capability while enhancing survivability through dispersed forward operations. In support of this objective, any factors adversely affecting a squadron's operational capability needed to be identified.[46]

The concept for Vapor Trail was conceptually simple but challenging for wing personnel. First, a DOB, DLA, and DPA for each squadron comprised the base complex for a dispersed wing. The execution of combat missions would occur only from the DOBs. DLAs would provide locations for further dispersal of aircraft but would not provide facilities to support combat operations. The DPAs would make available off-base parking areas to further disperse squadron aircraft. Deployable wing elements would consist of aircraft, pilots, minimum essential ground-support personnel, equipment, and supplies. For exercise purposes, enemy attack would put the peacetime wing (MOB) out of action. A rear-echelon base would supply aircraft parts and provide the principal maintenance. Mobile maintenance teams from the rear base would accomplish minor repairs at dispersed bases. In sum, Exercise Vapor Trail would not indicate the maximum rates of flying possible, but instead, would discover ways to sustain a satisfactory operational capability from dispersed bases.[47]

The 36th Fighter Wing at Bitburg AB, Germany, conducted Exercise Vapor Trail from 16 August to 30 September 1954. Each of the three squadrons of the wing—the 22nd, 23rd, and 53rd Fighter Squadrons—deployed initially to three separate DOBs at Giebelstadt, Neubiberg, and Wiesbaden. Subsequently, the three squadrons exercised three dispersed landing areas at Rhein-Main, Fürstenfeldbruck, and Stuttgart. Wing aircraft flew about 3,840 hours during the exercise, which is equivalent to a rate of about 2,500 hours per month. This total surpassed the average monthly rate flown by the wing during the rest of 1954 by about 40 percent. The average in-commission rate for the wing's F-86F aircraft during the exercise was about 78 percent. The average in-commission rate for the wing for the rest of the year was 71 percent. A rear-main base at Bordeaux, France, provided the principal maintenance and supply of aircraft parts. A combat operations center (COC) for the wing functioned at Neubiberg AB, Germany, which also served as a DOB. The office of the wing commander was at the wing COC. Throughout the exercise, overall operational control remained with the Twelfth Air Force air control center. The 36th Fighter Wing flew missions in support of air defense of the Twelfth Air Force area, ground control intercept training, air-to-ground gunnery missions, and other normal training missions.[48]

USAFE's operations analysis of Exercise Vapor Trail produced eight major recommendations concerning dispersed operations. First, war emergency stocks of recoverable and expendable aircraft parts needed to be pre-positioned in-theater for immediate use by dispersed bases. Second, the minimum maintenance capability of a squadron at a dispersed base should be the "crew chief" concept tested in the exercise. The crew chief concept allowed forward maintenance personnel to accomplish component changes, trouble-shooting, and minor repairs. Third, further exercises were needed to investigate the types of periodic inspections and major maintenance that dispersed bases could successfully accomplish. Fourth, in wartime, USAFE should not use the rear-echelon base concept for maintenance of two or more wings due to the vulnerability of a single base to atomic attack. Fifth, the USAF should actively support the Twelfth Air Force program of procuring and outfitting mobile vans. Subsequently, mobile-van–equipped wings should conduct training and exercises in base evacuation. Sixth, communication needed to be improved between dispersed bases. Seventh, additional testing of the aircraft trailer was needed. Eighth, future aircraft and weapon systems, together with their maintenance and support facilities, should incorporate mobility and dispersal design requirements.[49] Vapor Trail proved that logistics, maintenance, personnel, and procurement considerations are all potential vulnerabilities that will affect overall combat effectiveness if not properly addressed.

The *USAFE Operations Analysis Report* produced several major conclusions. First, the exercise clearly demonstrated the capability of a fighter wing to support an accelerated flying program from dispersed forward bases while supplied and maintained from a rear base. Second, the exercise did not test an emergency evacuation of a home base to a dispersed base. Future training and exercises in base evacuation were necessary to develop wing mobility, to determine transportation required to disperse a wing, and to assist in determining how much, if any, aircraft, supply, equipment, or personnel are required at dispersed bases during peacetime. Third, dispersal during wartime is necessary for survival. Fourth, the resupply of aircraft parts to dispersed bases is feasible by air during the night. Fifth, dispersed operations require more reliable, flexible, and secure communication systems than those of the exercise. Seventh, in peacetime, it is acceptable for dispersed operations to concentrate equipment, specialists, supply, and several aircraft from two or three wings at one rear main base. In contrast, during wartime, the concentration of logistical assets at only one location would make it a lucrative target for atomic attack. Several rear-echelon bases are required to ensure continuous operations at dispersed forward bases. Eighth, maintenance and support functions suffered due to not being originally designed for mobile and dispersed operations.[50] Overall, the dispersed operational concept proved a viable framework for increasing survivability and sustainability of combat forces. Similarly, a dispersed operational concept specifically designed for the Pacific Rim would offer many of the same advantages. The dispersed operational concept would increase the survivability of US military forces, increase the targeting difficulty of an adversary, signal commitment to US allies, and enhance overall US joint war-fighting capability.

Summary of USAFE's Lessons Learned

USAFE's experience in developing and exercising the USAFE dispersal program during the 1950s provides invaluable insights toward improving current and future concepts to defeat the looming antiaccess challenge in the Pacific Rim. These lessons learned are broken down into three specific categories: strategic, operational, and tactical.

Several significant strategic-level lessons learned, which directly apply to the Pacific Rim, emerged from the USAFE historic evidence. In developing military CONOPS, elements of strategic coercion, as applied to international relations, need to be clearly understood and enhanced.[51] An effective US coercive strategy must address deterrence, perceived US vulnerabilities, enemy counterstrategies, coercive diplomacy, and compellent military force options.

It is critical for the United States within any coercive strategy to deter the use of nuclear weapons. Deterrence typically seeks to clarify the adversarial actions that are to be deterred—that is, to specify the actions the deterrer will respond to by inflicting some form of punishment on the aggressor. This requires communication, military capability, and the will to use it. USAFE's dispersal program enhanced the survivability and operational capability of its combat assets by increasing the number of airfields able to conduct combat operations. By addressing the vulnerability and capability of its combat assets, USAFE directly affected the political and military viability of NATO. Thus, the USAFE dispersal plan conveyed the key aspects of coercion theory: credibility, commitment, and communications.[52]

Similarly, a Pacific Rim–dispersed CONOPS would demonstrate US credibility by enhancing the ability to operate within growing precision-guided ballistic and cruise missile threat rings. US willingness to accept similar risks as its Pacific Rim allies would signal to potential adversaries that any aggressive actions against the United States or its allies would bring the full weight of the United States against them. A US force posture shift toward the Pacific Rim would enhance the overall credibility of the United States and its allies to defend sovereign lands and interests from any acts of aggression. Conversely, these potential actions would assist in shaping the perceptions and actions of potential adversaries. In Western Europe during the 1950s, the Soviets were arguably deterred from employing a first-strike atomic strategy due to the increased survivability of USAFE forces capable of accomplishing significant retaliatory measures. Likewise, any potential adversary must consider the coercive effect of an enhanced US power-projection capability in-theater. Subsequently, the options for US coercive diplomacy grow as opportunities exist to exercise dispersed forward operations. In Europe, for example, dispersed operations enabled communicating intent during times of increased international tensions between East and West, such as the Cuban missile crisis.[53]

In October 1962, the USAFE dispersal program added an additional means by which Pres. John F. Kennedy could convey US resolve to the Soviets during the Cuban missile crisis. Kennedy believed the Soviets were placing missiles in Cuba to coerce US capitulation in West Berlin.[54] Therefore, the United States was not only considering appropriate actions to deal directly with the Soviet missiles in Cuba, but also to protect West Berlin from possible Soviet actions.

Fortunately, the United States had planned, implemented, and exercised the USAFE dispersal program and was prepared to execute it during a real-world crisis. USAFE's foresight in pushing for an operational answer to survive and operate within a threatened Western Europe proved prescient. As part of an overall display of military force and commitment during the missile crisis, USAFE executed its dispersal plan. Additionally, CINCUSAFE directed the execution of Operation Hawk Eye, which flowed fighter squadrons (F-84Fs, F-104Cs, and F-100Cs) further forward to improve strike force readiness and dispersal posture.[55] Historically, there are many facets to the US success in the Cuban missile crisis; the ability to defend West Berlin and signal, to the Soviets, US resolve through dispersal procedures is but one. Thus, at the strategic level of policy making, a dispersed operational concept provides national decision makers additional diplomatic leverage. The groundwork for conducting dispersal operations in Europe was laid in the mid-1950s, many years before the missile crisis. Similarly, the United States needs to prepare now for dispersal operations in the Pacific Rim in order to execute successful combat operations in the future.

Multiple operational-level lessons learned emerged from the USAFE historic evidence that directly impact considerations for the Pacific Rim. First, USAFE developed an effective framework for conducting dispersed operations that involved not only physical dispersal but also a multitude of passive defenses. The development of a similar framework in the Pacific Rim would greatly enhance the combat effectiveness of all military forces.

Second, USAFE revealed the critical importance of networking all units together to increase overall combat effectiveness. Networking involved several important aspects: command and control, communications, intelligence, transportation, supply, refueling, and munitions. The Pacific Rim requires significant networking of all these requirements due to the demanding geographical conditions. Yet, current command, control, communications, computers, intelligence, surveillance, and reconnaissance (C4ISR) capabilities provide incredible opportunities to overcome the tyranny of distance.

Third, USAFE recognized the importance of continually rotating all the units through dispersed locations. Currently, the USAF's AEF construct provides the potential for exercising dispersed operations in the Pacific Rim. Continual rotations in the Pacific theater would serve multiple purposes, such as exercising the dispersed CONOPS designed for actual combat operations; revealing unit weaknesses in conducting combat operations from a deployed location, especially jungle terrains; and maintaining individual proficiency in operating from remote bases and projecting combat power across vast distances.

Fourth, USAFE actions revealed the critical need for pre-positioning sufficient war materiel to conduct combat operations for several weeks prior to resupply. This lesson is especially important in the Pacific, again due to the geography. Proper amounts and types of war materiel need to be stored at forward locations from depots to DOBs. Fifth, dispersed operations make an adversary's targeting strategy inherently more difficult. By increasing basing options in the Pacific, potential adversaries will face a more difficult counterantiaccess challenge. Sixth, intratheater air mobility is a crucial force enhancer which requires meticulous management in a combat environment. Seventh, air defense is a significant capability when operating within threat rings. Eighth, planners can develop cost-effective measures for minimizing the cost of training personnel, supplying equipment, and maintaining facilities in support of dispersed operations. Ninth, desired capabilities should drive future weapon systems procurement. This becomes even more important in the Pacific Rim due to the vast distances and rugged terrain.

The USAFE historic evidence produced several important tactical-level lessons learned that are applicable to the Pacific Rim. First, the identification and incorporation of new technologies and capabilities can enhance local dispersed operations. In the Pacific Rim, the capability to protect forces at the base level incorporates several technologies such as GPS jammers, base missile defense systems, small surveillance unmanned aerial vehicles (UAV), and portable aircraft shelters. Second, passive defense measures can significantly increase the survivability of combat assets. Passive defense measures include hardened shelters, underground bunkers, camouflage, dispersal parking, and revetments. Third, when operating in threat rings, military forces must actively prepare for emergency evacuation of personnel and resources.

The ramifications of a viable dispersed CONOPS are immense. Fortunately, USAFE's efforts in the 1950s to enhance the survivability and operational combat effectiveness of its combat wings provide ample lessons, which can be directly applied to future considerations in the Pacific. The next chapter addresses efforts by SAC to counter vulnerabilities or antiaccess challenges.

Notes

1. Harry S. Truman, *Years of Trial and Hope* (Garden City, NY: Doubleday & Co., 1956), 306–7.

2. Thomas K. Finletter, *Power and Policy: US Foreign Policy and Military Power in the Hydrogen Age* (New York: Harcourt, Brace and Co., 1954), 377.

3. Everett C. Dolman, *Astropolitik: Classical Geopolitics in the Space Age* (London, Frank Cass Publishers, 2002), 89.

4. See Robert F. Futrell, *Volume I, Ideas, Concepts, Doctrine: Basic Thinking in the United States Air Force, 1907–1960* (Maxwell AFB, AL: Air University Press, December 1989), 304. Futrell encapsulates Gen Hoyt S. Vandenberg's four principal events that were instrumental in releasing the strings to the budget purse: (1) explosion of the atomic bomb by the Soviets; (2) North Korean invasion of South Korea; (3) US commitment to assist in the defense of Western Europe; (4) calculation of the Joint Chiefs of Staff that by mid-1954 the USSR would possess such an atomic weapons arsenal as to threaten all of the United States. Futrell's account is based on Vandenberg's "Valedictory of the Chief," *Air Force Magazine*, July 1953, 6.

5. Irving B. Holley Jr., "The Evolution of Operations Research and Its Impact on the Military Establishment; The Air Force Experience," in *Science, Technology, and Warfare, Proceedings of the Third Military History Symposium, United States Air Force Academy, 8–9 May 1969*, eds. Monte D. Wright and Lawrence J. Paszek (Washington, DC: Office of Air Force History and Air Force Academy, 1970), 100.

6. See chaps. 1–3 of John Lewis Gaddis, *We Now Know: Rethinking Cold War History* (Oxford, UK: Clarendon Press, 1997), for a more complete analysis on how the Cold War struggle between the United States and the USSR emerged and developed with the eventual creation of a bipolar system.

7. See USAFE Historical Monograph Series 1974, no. 3. *USAFE and the Commitment to NATO, 1949–1973* (Office of History, Headquarters United States Air Forces in Europe, 1974). The North Atlantic Treaty committed the 12 signatory nations (Belgium, Canada, Denmark, France, Iceland, Italy, Luxembourg, the Netherlands, Norway, Portugal, the United Kingdom, and the United States) to take measures to improve individual and collective defense and to resist an attack on any member.

8. It is important to define several of the terms used in this study. First, *coercion* is the use of threatened force, including the limited use of actual force to back up the threat, to induce an adversary to behave differently than it otherwise would. Coercion can involve the threat or actual use of military force, economic sanctions, or a range of other political pressures. Additionally, there can be promises and rewards as well as threats and punishments. Coercive strategy needs to capture the distinction of focusing on the use of threatened force to manipulate the adversary's choices. Subsequently, coercion is further divided into two subgroups, deterrence and compellence. *Deterrence* is making the adversary not do something it might otherwise do; it is about preserving the status quo. Lastly, *compellence* involves attempts to reverse an action that has already occurred or to otherwise overturn the status quo. For an excellent short read on these concepts, see Karl Mueller, "Coercion and Air Power: A Primer for the Military Strategist" (paper presented at the Royal Netherlands Air Force Air Power Colloquium, Netherlands Defense Staff College, The Hague, 6 June 2000).

9. USAFE document, "Reduction of USAFE Tactical and Logistical Vulnerability," (USAFE: 15 January 1955), 1. This document's short title, "USAFE Dispersal Program," will be used hereafter for citation purposes.

10. *History of Headquarters United States Air Forces in Europe: 1 July–1 December 1954*, vol. 1. Office of Information Services, Headquarters, Historical Division, USAFE, 1956 (Hereafter: *USAFE History, 1954*), 61.

11. "USAFE Dispersal Program," Introduction.

12. Ibid., Annex A, Concept of Operations.

13. Ibid., foreword.

14. *USAFE History, 1954*, 61–63

15. Ibid., 63.

16. "USAFE Dispersal Program," 63.

17. A DOB was a dispersal base from which combat flying operations were conducted. A DLA was a dispersal base that provided a secondary dispersed operational base for fur-

ther dispersal of aircraft, as required. A DPA was a parking area for aircraft to be taxied or towed from that allowed for dispersed hiding. See "USAFE Dispersal Program," 63.

18. "USAFE Dispersal Program," 61–63.

19. See USAFE's "Program for Dispersal of Aircraft and Related Requirements, USAFE Tactical Bases, Germany, Fiscal Year 1955, DM Program," no date (1952).

20. Ibid.

21. See section of "USAFE Dispersal Program," Program for Dispersal of Aircraft and Related Requirements, 1954.

22. *USAFE History, 1954*, 66–67.

23. Ibid., 67–68. The team consisted of Col C. R. Opper, Lt Col J. C. Peaslee, and Maj John D. Macklin Jr., all from the Office of ACS/Opns, and Col J. W. Thompson of the Office of ACS/Instal.

24. Col Frederic H. Fairchild, acting chief of Plans Division of USAFE, to Brig Gen Royden E. Beebe, USAFE ACS/Opns, memorandum, 1 June 1954, subj: Base Complex for Dispersal in France.

25. Ibid.

26. Lt Col J. C. Peaslee, USAFE OACS/Opns, Plans Div, to USAFE ACS/Opns and COFS, letter, 2 July 1954, subj: NATO-USAF Officer Exchange; and Report of Lt Col J. C. Peaslee.

27. Ibid.

28. HQ USAF to all major commands, letter, 9 July 1954, subj: Vulnerability of Tactical Forces.

29. *USAFE History, 1954*, 70.

30. Ibid., 71.

31. See Memo, subj: Dispersal Plan, 17 June 1954, in *USAFE History, 1954*, vol. 8.

32. Lt Gen W. H. Tunner to Commander, Twelfth Air Force, letter, 30 July 1954, subj: Development and Implementation of Dispersed Operational Concept.

33. *USAFE History, 1954*, 74.

34. USAFE Asst DCS/Opns to Twelfth Air Force, letter, 4 October 1954, subj: Selection of Bases for Development to Improve Dispersal Capabilities.

35. *USAFE History, 1954*, 76.

36. See Memo for Col M. E. Marston, signed by Col Oren J. Poage, C/Temporary Dispersal Program Committee, 30 December 1954, subj: Revision of USAFE Dispersal Program.

37. See Attachment to Memo for Col M. E. Marston, subj: General Tunner's Summation of the Discussion Held at a Meeting, 29 December 1954, HQ USAFE, Main Conference Room, USAFE Dispersal Program.

38. Message, EOOTS-T-5272, CINCUSAFE to CINCUSAREUR and US CINCEUR, 3 August 1954.

39. Message EOOTS-T-7084, CINCUSAFE to US CINCEUR, 23 September 1954.

40. Maj Gen John F. Uncles, USAREUR COFS, to CG Seventh Army, letter, 29 December 1954, subj: Air Defense Planning.

41. Lt Col M. H. Culp (AMFE Director of Engineering), interview by Dr. W. F. Sprague (USAFE Historical Division, Office of Information Services), 29 June 1955.

42. Capt C. S. Hoster (USAFE ODCS/Opns), interview by Dr. W. F. Sprague, 28 June 1955.

43. Culp, interview.

44. See Message EOAC-7960, CINCUSAFE to Commander Twelfth Air Force, 15 October 1954.

45. Col William J. Bell, USAFE ODCS/Opns, to Commander Twelfth Air Force, letter, 8 December 1954, subj: USAFE Dispersal Program.

46. See the HQ USAFE Operations Analysis Report No. 1, *VAPOR TRAIL—An Exercise in Dispersed Operation*, by Arthur H. Peterson, USAFE operations analyst (Headquarters USAFE, Germany, 14 March 1955), 1–2. Hereafter: USAFE Operations Analysis Report No. 1.

47. Ibid., 8–9.

48. Ibid., 10–17.

49. Ibid., 3–4.

50. Ibid., 5–7.

51. For an excellent presentation on coercion theory, read Daniel Byman and Matthew Waxman, *The Dynamics of Coercion* (New York: Cambridge University Press, 2002).

52. According to Karl Mueller in "Coercion and Air Power: A Primer for the Military Strategist," (paper presented at the Royal Netherlands Air Force Air Power Colloquium, Netherlands Defense Staff College, The Hague, 6 June 2000), 6–7, the three Cs of coercion are credibility, capability, and communication. Credibility—a threat will only carry coercive weight to the degree that the adversary believes the coercer will actually carry it out if compliance is not forthcoming. Capability—if the adversary does not believe that the coercer has the ability to carry out a coercive threat, it is worthless as a coercive instrument, even if the coercer's will to try is not in doubt. Communication—threats must be communicated in order to be effective; a difficult proposition if the messages involved are complex and the coercer wishes to send them through actions rather than words.

53. See USAFE's dispersal actions during the Cuban missile crisis in *Chronology of the Cuban Missile Crisis, 6 October thru 24 November 1962*, USAFE, 1962.

54. Graham Allison and Philip Zelikow, *Essence of Decision: Explaining the Cuban Missile Crisis* (New York: Addison-Wesley Educational Publishers, 1999), 100–109.

55. *United States Air Forces in Europe, Chronology of the Cuban Missile Crisis*, 6 October thru 24 November 1962. (USAFE, 1962), 17.

Chapter 4

SAC—Operating on Reflex in the '50s

A deterrent strategy is aimed at a rational enemy. Without a deterrent, general war is likely. With it, however, war might still occur. This is one reason deterrence is only a part and not the whole of a military and foreign policy.

—Albert Wohlstetter, 5 January 1960

(A deterrent force is) an effective nuclear offensive force which is secure from (total) destruction by the enemy regardless of what offensive and defensive action he takes against it.

—Gen Curtis LeMay, 1956

What would happen if a first-strike package of ballistic and cruise missiles rained down on US bases in the Pacific Rim? Moreover, how would the capability to accomplish a crippling first strike affect our policies toward Pacific Rim nations? These are central questions permeating the antiaccess challenge. Similarly, in the 1950s, high-level leaders and analysts were asking, what if the Soviets launched a first strike with their burgeoning nuclear missile forces? What if the Soviets specifically designed their first-strike capability to attack SAC's nuclear forces? Could SAC survive such an attack and, equally important, mount a credible counterattack, thus deterring the incentive for the Soviets to strike first?[1] Just as the increasing antiaccess threat will continue to dominate US defense thinking, these questions dominated US security concerns throughout the 1950s. This chapter explores the contemporary relevance of how the United States confronted the growing threat to its nuclear striking power in the 1950s.

Throughout the 1950s and early 1960s, the United States diversified and strengthened its nuclear capabilities by developing a strategic triad of long-range bombers, ICBMs and IRBMs, and submarine-launched ballistic missiles (SLBM). During this era, the United States developed its strategic nuclear forces from a purely air-based operation to a more survivable triad. The strategic triad was deemed capable of surviving any enemy aggression, providing a diversity of responses, and being coercive in its perceived threat. The development of the strategic triad enabled the United States to retain a deterrent nuclear force that was survivable, responsive, sustainable, and mobile. Likewise, the advantages of fielding diverse conventional force-employment methods (long-range bombers, close-in tactical airpower, nuclear-powered guided missile submarines [SSGN] and maritime, ground, and special forces) in the Pacific Rim will only enhance the overall combat effectiveness of US military forces in the future. Additionally, a strong, diversified force posture in the Pacific Rim will achieve multiple advantages: greater political and diplomatic options, a stronger display of commitment to US allies, greater interservice security, and decreased strategic options and increased targeting difficulties for potential adversaries. The development of the strategic triad in the 1950s shows the strength of diversifying our power-projection capabilities.

After World War II, forward basing was the initial US strategy to contain Soviet expansion into Western Europe.[2] These bases were located throughout Western Europe, primarily in the United Kingdom, West Germany, France, and Spain. US access and usage of these overseas bases directly supported the geostrategic containment concept encapsulated in the Truman Doctrine and the military buildup recommended in NSC-68, a study conducted by an ad hoc group of State Department and Defense Department personnel in response to the Soviet atomic weapon detonation in September 1949.[3] It advocated an immediate, large-scale increase in US military strength to provide a sufficient military shield capable of resisting local Soviet aggressions in Europe and deterring general war.[4] Thus, the United States, with support from NATO host nations, undertook a massive development of overseas basing facilities.

During this stressful time, concern over SAC's increasingly vulnerable basing structure came to the attention of the Joint Chiefs of Staff think tank, called the Weapons Systems Evaluation Group, in February 1950. The group reported, in remarkably direct language, that SAC's bases in England were vulnerable to being "Pearl Harbored at the outset of future hostilities." Additionally, the Joint Intelligence Committee supported this analysis by proclaiming that if the Soviets launched a preemptive first strike, it could be sufficient to seriously damage US overseas bases.[5] Yet, initially, few senior SAC commanders took these reports seriously. Instead, they focused their efforts on taking the offense and the initiative. Their priority goals were penetrating enemy defenses and attacking enemy targets. Minor thought was given to the survivability and sustainability of the bases from which these strike forces would launch. Furthermore, the military was slowly analyzing the impact on base vulnerability created by the introduction of Soviet atomic weapon capability in 1949. By 1952 SAC was still fixated on forward basing its medium-range bombers, with plans to expand to 82 bases. In contrast, RAND analyst Albert Wohlstetter viewed base vulnerability as central to the strategic problem associated with strike operations in Europe.[6]

Wohlstetter spearheaded RAND's efforts in producing a USAF-sponsored study on the selection and use of overseas bases. He combined two central facts to buttress his argument: all of the bases in Europe were within range of Soviet medium bombers and, hence, the potential delivery of atomic weapons. Based on a systems-analysis approach, Wohlstetter concluded that as few as 120 40-kiloton bombs, with an average miss distance of 4,000 feet, could destroy 75–85 percent of the B-47 bombers at overseas bases. Furthermore, he viewed the basing scheme as destabilizing. SAC was extremely vulnerable to a Soviet first-strike attack, thus creating such a lucrative target as to invite Soviet preemptive action.[7]

Based on this logic, Wohlstetter provided several recommendations to enhance the survivability of the SAC bomber force, including improvement of advanced early warning radar systems; use of overseas bases for refueling only; dispersal of supplies; hardening of facilities; bolstering of air defense squadrons; and better protection of repair facilities.[8] From this list, the priority recommendation became moving the bombers to CONUS locations and using overseas bases for refueling operations only.

The RAND analysis generated significant debate in the USAF, culminating in the Fullhouse Concept, a plan developed by Col Ed Jones at MacDill AFB, Florida, on how best to operationally employ B-47s from the CONUS. The concept attempted to limit the use of overseas bases to only en route aerial refueling and poststrike recovery. Thus, SAC bombers could strike potential Soviet targets from the United States with decreased but still critical reliance on overseas bases.[9] The key analytic point was that even though bombers may be pulled back to CONUS bases, the strike concept still relied on secure forward basing.

Although the RAND study initiated considerable debate within SAC regarding reliance on vulnerable overseas bases, SAC did not adopt its recommendations. The study did catalyze a DOD debate that SAC would eventually lose due to the clear logic of Wohlstetter's analysis. According to Wohlstetter, "It is clear not only that an invulnerable SAC is a deterrent but also that a vulnerable SAC is an urgent invitation."[10] For many analysts, Soviet perceptions of a successful first strike capable of devastating the US strategic force dramatically heightened the chances of war.

Subsequently, the development of Soviet ICBMs increased the need for analyzing SAC's vulnerability even if it were to fly its bombers only from CONUS bases. The United States would not be the sanctuary envisioned when developing the B-52 for long-range strike operations. The threat ring created by ICBMs enveloped the entire globe—no place was going to remain safe from potential attack.

Wohlstetter and another RAND analyst, Fred Hoffman, analyzed the defense of SAC against the developing Soviet ICBM threat. In 1954 they concluded "the defenses programmed, or recommended, to protect SAC in the 1950s will be entirely ineffective against an ICBM which would deliver bombs with essentially no warning. It now appears this weapon may be feasible for the Russians by the end of this period [the 1950s]."[11]

RAND made several recommendations for reducing SAC's vulnerability to ICBM attack, including hardened shelters, local base dispersal, blast protection, multiplication of bases, separation of bases by significant distances, and underground shelters—remarkably similar to the conclusions reached by USAFE during the same period. Within the CONUS, the study primarily advocated that SAC use hardened shelters dispersed in clusters. Additional analysis depicted the cost effectiveness of investing in hardened shelters versus leaving bombers unprotected against even a small ICBM attack.[12]

These arguments influenced Air Force leadership in expanding forces to a proposed 137 wings and building needed bases in the northern tier of the United States for transpolar, intercontinental air missions. Yet, even with in-flight refueling, medium-range B-47s required forward basing overseas to accomplish their missions into the Soviet Union. Additionally, in 1956 Gen Curtis LeMay proposed that only a single B-52 squadron and a single B-47 wing be located at each base. This proposal increased the overall security of forces and significantly complicated enemy targeting requirements.[13]

The USAF accepted the intent of dispersing bomber assets across multiple air bases, but due to financial constraints was unable to achieve total dispersal per LeMay's recommendation. However, the USAF designated 80 to 100 alternate airfields for B-47 dispersal during increased periods of international tension.[14] Recognizing the increasing threat posed by Soviet bombers, atomic weapons, and development of IRBM and ICBM capabilities, SAC hastened efforts to increase survivability of its strategic bomber force.

Although LeMay had resisted early RAND analyses, by the mid-1950s he clearly recognized the increasing vulnerability of overseas bases to attack from Soviet medium-range bombers and IRBMs.[15] SAC began developing multiple measures to decrease the vulnerability of air bases, first recognizing the need for an early warning system. The Distant Early Warning (DEW) Line became operational on 15 February 1954. SAC built the DEW Line as the primary air defense warning in case of an over-the-pole invasion of North America. It considered an attack over the North Pole by enemy nuclear bombers and missiles a real threat to the security of the United States. The DEW Line was established across the tundra of northern Greenland, Canada, and Alaska, with radar stations providing overlapping coverage and the ability to detect aircraft and missiles within their areas of surveillance. Second, with the emergence of IRBMs and ICBMs, warning time decreased dramatically to 15 minutes in the CONUS. As early as 1956, LeMay began pushing his bomber wings toward a hair-trigger alert capability, designed to launch as many aircraft as possible within the 15-minute window. Third, LeMay aggressively advocated building more B-52s and KC-135s to facilitate intercontinental capability. SAC needed to develop new capabilities, longer-range bombers, and more-capable tankers to accommodate the new basing construct.

Fourth, SAC agreed to base all bombers in the CONUS, withdrawing them from forward locations. Yet, the process of withdrawing required time to build appropriate bases and facilities and to produce B-52s to replace the shorter-range B-47s. Once SAC made the decision to move all its bombers into CONUS locations, significant adjustments to operational concepts needed to occur.[16] During this transition, SAC needed to increase the survivability of its bomber force while maintaining the capability to strike targets in the Soviet Union. It began an operational concept called Reflex Action to answer this issue. Prior to implementing Reflex Action,

SAC had deployed entire bomb wings on extended rotations to overseas bases as a deterrent to the Soviet Union. Due to increasing Soviet strike capability, this was no longer feasible.

SAC implemented Reflex Action in July 1957 by deploying small elements of aircraft to forward bases where they were ready to react within minutes to an overt attack. Reflex Action involved mainly overseas bases. These bases played a significant part in SAC strike plans until it acquired sufficient heavy bombers, tankers, and ICBMs to launch its entire effort from the CONUS. This forward base dispersal increased the number of weapons the enemy would require to launch a successful attack, and the bases increased the probability of SAC receiving an early attack warning.[17] Reflex Action was an operational concept with the expeditionary employment of airpower as its foundational principle. In sum, Reflex Action was an intermediary operational concept SAC implemented to bridge the transition from forward, overseas basing to CONUS basing of its long-range bombers.

Sidi Slimane AB, French Morocco, became the SAC proving ground for Reflex Action operations. Reflex Action commenced with four Second Air Force wings sending five B-47s each to Sidi Slimane. This new operations system relied on the premise that a smaller contingent of crews and aircraft on ground alert would be more efficient than maintaining entire wings at these bases on 90-day rotational training assignments. If successful, SAC planned to replace the 90-day rotational program at all overseas bases with the Reflex Action operational concept. Then, crews and aircraft would begin more frequent rotations from CONUS bases to overseas locations.

Operation Reflex Action—Sidi Slimane Test

SAC believed a small contingency of aircraft and crews maintained in readiness at all times in the forward area would provide greater combat effectiveness and efficiency than the wing rotation concept.[18] The Second Air Force staff, under the direction of its commander, Maj Gen George Mundy, began planning for the implementation of the operational concept five months prior to the test. SAC began Reflex Action on 1 July 1957 at Sidi Slimane.[19] Initially, SAC planners designed the Sidi Slimane test to last six months with a bare-base build-up phase, an operational employment phase, and a gradual development to an alert posture phase.

Overall, the Sidi Slimane test succeeded in proving the operational feasibility of the Reflex Action concept. After witnessing the early phases of the test, Col Julian M. Bleyer, commander of the 305th Bomb Wing (BW), stated that Reflex Action "seemed well planned," functioned "much better than many similar type programs [he had] observed in the past;" and, finally, "this is the type operation for which Jet Bombardment has been striving."[20] Yet, just as Exercise Vapor Trail taught USAFE how to refine its dispersal concept, the Sidi Slimane test revealed lessons that led to important changes.

The initial problems encountered at the forward base dealt more with the quality of living conditions than with operational considerations. Three of the bomb wings reported inadequate housing and messing facilities. Commanders routinely violated planned schedules for crews and maintenance personnel. Commanders consistently required "off-duty" crews to report to the flight line to assist in preparing the aircraft. The initial operational conditions severely strained maintenance personnel, causing degradation in capability. Specifically, the 306th and 379th Bomb Wings reported maintenance "limited" and "marginal" in July.[21] While supporting a 24/7 operation, several of the enlisted maintenance personnel worked 80- to 90-hour weeks. Additionally, some ground support vehicles, such as alert jeeps, fell into serious disrepair.[22] However, none of these discrepancies created any insurmountable difficulties in the employment of Reflex Action. In fact, with increasing operational experience, Sidi Slimane personnel eliminated the problems associated with initial operations.[23] The exercise not only refined procedures, but also demonstrated that SAC units could adapt rapidly to expeditionary operations.

On 1 October 1957, a now-ready Sidi Slimane force began 30-minute alert operations. That same month, the Headquarters SAC director of Materiel, Maj Gen J. D. Ryan (who later became the USAF chief of staff), visited the Moroccan area. He informed Gen Thomas S. Power, CINCSAC, that he "was highly impressed with the ease of operation." General Ryan noted that units were able to maintain 19.4 (out of 20) aircraft in commission to accomplish the mission.[24] Similarly, in November, Colonel Bleyer proclaimed, "It appears that most of the problems pertinent to the Reflex Operation have been eliminated."[25] Crews of the 306th BW believed "without exception, that REFLEX ACTION is the most effective, practical, best planned, and coordinated EWP Plan."[26] Crews that rotated through Sidi Slimane felt that Reflex Action finally gave them the kind of readiness the Americans expected from SAC.[27] As an expeditionary concept, Reflex Action proved highly effective in expanding a bare base into a fully operational overseas bomber wing.

Reflex Action had some limitations in the context of overall SAC operations, however. According to Fifth Air Division commander Brig Gen K. K. Compton, placing materiel, facilities, and manpower in the forward area to support anything but alert forces and poststrike recovery was neither consistent with the threat nor with sound tactical planning. He recommended SAC adopt several operational changes as follows: (1) modify the SAC War Plan to limit forward bases to Reflex Action operations and poststrike staging only; (2) adjust base stocks, facilities, and manpower to fit these missions; (3) rotate alert forces as often as possible; (4) maintain a core team of forward area maintenance and operations support personnel on a six-month rotation; and (5) begin rotating weapons with alert forces as soon as possible.[28]

After careful examination of various CONUS alert forces' operations, SAC decided that the Sidi Slimane force was the most effective. SAC concluded that the Reflex Action operational concept would continue to expand, commensurate with its capability to provide air refueling and temporary duty personnel.[29] Although the Sidi Slimane operation was initially a six-month test, it proved such a success that SAC extended it indefinitely, and all future SAC expeditionary planning would emulate the Sidi Slimane model. By the end of 1957, and stimulated by the Sputnik surprise launch that illuminated the growing missile threat, SAC planned to expand the Reflex Action operational concept to all bases in North Africa; one base in Spain—Zaragoza; and by early 1958, into two Royal Air Force (RAF) bases in the United Kingdom (UK)—Greenham Common and Fairford.[30]

Expansion of Operation Reflex Action

Due to its operational success, SAC expanded the Reflex Action concept on 1 January 1958 to three additional overseas bases and three northern US bases. The 2nd, 308th, and 384th BWs began rotating to RAF Fairford; the 98th, 307th, and 310th BWs flew to RAF Greenham Common; and the 22nd, 43rd, and 320th BWs sent detachments to Eielson AFB, Alaska. Also, the 19th BW replaced the 308th at Sidi Slimane.

SAC also implemented elements of Reflex Action at their ever-expanding CONUS bases. Units of the Fifteenth and Second Air Forces went on alert at northern bases of the Eighth Air Force. The 509th BW at Walker AFB, New Mexico, sent five aircraft to Pease AFB, New Hampshire; the 97th BW at Biggs AFB, Texas, moved aircraft to Plattsburgh AFB, New York; and the 44th BW at Lake Charles AFB, Louisiana, and the 321st BW at Pinecastle AFB, Florida, each maintained three aircraft at Loring AFB, Maine.[31]

Additional changes in February and April 1958 accomplished a further dispersal of the overseas alert force. On 18 February, SAC expanded North African operations by sending the 379th BW to Benguerir AB, Morocco, and the 305th BW to Nouasser AB, Morocco. On 1 April, the 306th BW began operations at Zaragoza AB, Spain, and the 2nd and 308th BWs moved their alert forces to RAF Brize Norton, UK, leaving only the 384th at RAF Fairford.[32] Reflex Action became firmly embedded as the SAC-dispersed operational concept for answering the expanding Soviet offensive threat. It was SAC's operational framework for countering the Soviet threat until it had sufficient long-range bombers, tankers, and ICBMs to conduct nuclear operations primarily from the CONUS. However, the USAF recognized that overseas bases would remain tremendously important, both in grand strategy and operationally as "jumping-off" places for highly mobile forces to combat wars of a limited nature.[33] SAC planners predicted that in the event of tactical warning, only those aircraft on an alert status could provide a sufficient retaliatory capability. Based on this analysis, SAC decided to maintain only an alert force overseas due to the necessity of attacking Soviet targets as soon as possible after initial warning, the limited number of tankers available at CONUS bases, and the advantages of dispersed locations, which increased targeting difficulties for an attacker attempting a surprise attack.[34] Reflex Action forces could strike targets in the Soviet Union and accomplish poststrike recovery at friendly bases without refueling when positioned at forward bases. In the year following its test run at Sidi Slimane, the Reflex Action concept expanded to eight overseas bases and three CONUS bases. Although Reflex Action's operations demanded a rigorous schedule of deployment and redeployment, crews generally favored it because of its realistic contribution to SAC's deterrent posture.[35]

Enhancing Forward-Dispersed Operations

Beginning in July 1958, SAC began the increased dispersal of its overseas Reflex Action forces to further enhance the survivability of its forces. SAC continued to expand the number of bases used and sent fewer aircraft to any one base, deciding on this course of action for two primary reasons. First, dispersed operations increased the number of weapons the enemy must launch for a successful attack. Second, dispersed operations increased the probability of SAC receiving an early warning of attack.[36] Any bomber unit deployed in support of Reflex Action operations immediately became part of the overseas base alert force upon landing. As soon as an incoming B-47 parked, maintenance crews began "cocking" procedures. The aircraft was expeditiously placed onto alert status within several hours.[37]

Throughout 1958 and 1959, SAC further dispersed its bomber force overseas. Starting 1 April 1958, it began sending Reflex Action deployments to Spanish bases for the first time: Zaragoza AB (306th BW), Torrejon AB (305th BW), and Moron AB (384th BW). In the UK, RAF Mildenhall entered the program in July, receiving aircraft from the 310th BW. In January 1959, Reflex Action expanded extensively in the UK, establishing operations at RAF Chelveston (301st BW), RAF Upper Heyford (98th BW), and RAF Bruntingthorpe (110th BW). In Alaska, SAC sent six aircraft to Eielson AFB from the 22nd and 320th BWs in July 1958, and on 8 January, an element of the 341st BW went to Elmendorf AFB. Within the CONUS, the 321st BW sent four aircraft to Loring AFB, Maine, and the 97th BW sent six to Plattsburgh AFB, New York.[38]

SAC also based tanker forces overseas along the en route corridors flown by deploying and redeploying Reflex Action bombers. On the northern route, it used bases at Harmon, Newfoundland; Goose Bay, Labrador; and Elmendorf and Eielson AFBs in Alaska. On the southern route, tankers were located at Kindley AFB, Bermuda, and Lajes Field, Azores. As a significant part of the operational viability of Reflex Action, KC-97 tankers were integral in supplying the fuel necessary to accomplish the missions.[39]

By the end of June 1959, the Reflex Action operation was two years old. It had progressed from a small test force at Sidi Slimane AB, French Morocco, to an extensive 18-base operation. By June 1958, bomber units no longer cited operational problems, such as substandard facilities, excessive overtime, or erratic schedules, as major issues. Although, the Reflex Action operational concept was built as an expeditionary, alert-oriented, defensive framework, it enhanced SAC's offensive capability. SAC could launch its strategic bomber force with only a 15-minute advance warning. This facilitated not only the survivability of the strategic force but also an immediate retaliatory hammer. Therefore, the Reflex Action concept presented the Soviets with an acute dilemma. If they attempted a surprise attack, they would unquestionably incur a certain number of retaliatory strikes. Thus, a Soviet first-strike decision would entail an assessment of value gained versus the certitude of overwhelming and catastrophic damage. If SAC counterstrikes were ever perceived as weak or weakening, the Soviets could decide to attack, confident they could attain victory. Hence, the United States needed to create a deterrent margin based both on Soviet capabilities and perceptions.[40]

In June 1959, Reflex Action immeasurably increased SAC's deterrent strength. SAC strived to put as many bombers and tankers within these rotations as possible. In reality, deployable SAC assets constituted an elite force. At each Reflex Action base, combat aircraft and crews stood poised and fully loaded, ready for the signal to launch. By July 1960, SAC war plans required one-third of the force to be capable of launching within 15 minutes. Since October 1957, SAC officially maintained aircraft on alert.[41] Yet, there was a possibility that at the same time it reached its goal of one-third, the concept would require modification. Ground alert required at least 15 minutes' warning to be successful. As long as the Soviets relied on aircraft, SAC would keep its edge; however, by 1960, missiles began to attain a more prominent place in the Soviet weapons inventory.

In mid-1959, the future of the Reflex Action operational concept seemed solid, as SAC funded all of the facilities for the ground-alert portion. However, SAC determined a need to reduce the number of aircraft maintained overseas due to the inherent vulnerability of these bases to ballistic missile attack. Nonetheless, the concept of alert dispersal—placing fewer aircraft on any one base—would continue. By the end of 1959, SAC represented the strongest nuclear strike force in the world because it had adapted to Soviet breakthroughs in nuclear weaponry and delivery systems. Yet, it would continue to become increasingly vulnerable to destruction as Soviet missile capabilities developed. Ironically, as SAC attempted to move more of its strategic force stateside, the Soviet nuclear threat rings would envelop any perceived safe havens. In sum, the global destructive power of Soviet nuclear arsenals denied the United States any sanctuaries from nuclear attack. The question remained, then and now, how best to operate within threat rings capable of destroying your forces.

Insights gained from Reflex Action directly apply to the Pacific Rim. In the future, the United States will require its long-range bombers to forward deploy toward potential regions of conflict. The requirement for long-range bombers to forward deploy during times of crisis generates two immediate access challenges in the Pacific Rim. First, the United States needs to maintain a balance between staging long-range bombers as far forward as possible to maximize their firepower potential versus protecting these valuable assets. Chapter 5 attempts to answer this equation, as the use of long-range bombers as part of the military's overall comprehensive access answer is pivotal. Second, the operating range of long-range bombers will drive tanker requirements and the need for intermediate recovery bases. Both considerations require maintaining land-based access within current threat-ring ranges.

Presently, basing long-range bombers only within the CONUS during conflicts diminishes US combat effectiveness. The long-range bombers must forward deploy in order to achieve sustainable and persistent power projection. From a nuclear mind-set of the 1950s and 1960s, SAC could justify its placement of long-range bombers stateside due to the perception that the nuclear missions would not demand long-term sortie regeneration; a nuclear conflict would be short and devastating. This SAC perspective has lost relevancy. Long-range bombers need to generate multiple sorties over long periods of time at the conventional level of war, as demonstrated in all US major conflicts requiring airpower.

Long-range bombers are and will remain an immensely important part of any US war-fighting capability. For the long-range bomber force to maintain its combat potency, the USAF needs to enhance several aspects of their employment. First, it needs to exercise the long-range bombers' expeditionary, alert, and dispersed operational capability. Otherwise, insights gained from previous experience will erode. Second, it needs to more clearly incorporate dispersal and alert lessons into joint and USAF doctrine. SAC developed Reflex Action as an operational concept designed to retain the bomber forces' deterrent quality. Reflex Action achieved this objective by enhancing the survivability of the bomber force through dispersal, alert, and early warning procedures. Similarly, in the 1950s, the USAF addressed how to field ballistic missile systems that were survivable from Soviet attack.

One Global Threat Ring

The emergence of nuclear ballistic missiles radically altered US foreign policy and military strategy. In 1954 the Teapot Committee, a group of scientists led by John von Neumann, examined the impact of potentially combining thermonuclear warheads with strategic missiles and the threat of the Soviets possessing this technology.[42] The official committee report submitted to the Congress on 10 February ominously stated:

> Unusual urgency for a strategic missile capability can arise from one of two principal causes: A rapid strengthening of the Soviet defenses against our SAC manned bombers, or rapid progress by the Soviet in his own development of strategic missiles which would provide a compelling political and psychological reason for our own effort to proceed apace. The former is to be expected during the second half of this decade. As to the latter . . . evidence exists of an appreciation in this field on the parts of the Soviets . . . it is natural to connect with the objective of development by the Soviets of intercontinental missiles.[43]

The Teapot Committee recommended an accelerated development program for building ICBMs within a six-year window. The USAF supported the recommendation and, in May 1954, selected Brig Gen Bernard A. Schriever to spearhead the Atlas ICBM program.[44] From this impetus, the Air Force would oversee development of the Atlas, Titan, and Minuteman ICBM programs, and the Navy would supervise the Polaris IRBM program. In the years following the decision to make the ICBM the nation's top defense priority, a specific review of the survivability design concepts incorporated into these weapon systems offers valuable lessons on how to operationally field vulnerable capabilities in a high-threat environment. How the United States addressed the vulnerability concerns of fielding ICBM units parallels current concerns on how to protect fixed airfields within precision threat rings. During the development phases of the ICBM programs, designers took specific actions to decrease the vulnerability of the weapon systems.

The search for survivable ICBM operational concepts began almost simultaneously with developing and fielding an ICBM. Perceptions existed among operators and scientists that recognized the eventual vulnerability of fixed targets to advanced technologies capable of delivering high-yield nuclear weapons. In the beginning, ICBM development focused primarily on the technical considerations required to merely achieve an intercontinental missile capability. In its aggressive pursuit of an ICBM capability, the United States recognized two distinct advantages in diversifying its employment methods for delivering nuclear weapons. First, if one mode of nuclear delivery fails, the other modes can still function and succeed. Second, diverse, independent modes of delivery severely complicated an adversary's ability to defeat all options. In the late 1950s, the ICBM race between the United States and the Soviet Union represented a critical quest for gaining the advantage in a deadly international fight for coercive control of the adversary through nuclear threats. Likewise, the advantages of fielding diverse conventional force-employment methods (long-range bombers, close-in tactical airpower, maritime forces, special forces, and ground forces) today will only enhance the overall future combat effectiveness of US military forces.

The race to field an ICBM system involved difficult decisions centered on several significant criteria: operational feasibility, cost, time, and survivability. This study focuses on ICBM survivability criteria, which includes three main factors: susceptibility, independence, and endurance. First, the susceptibility factor required that ICBMs be designed to survive potential Soviet threats. In particular, they needed to survive the eventual Soviet capability to deliver an ICBM with a high-yield nuclear weapon with sufficient accuracy. Second, the independence factor called for ICBM survivability regardless of the status of other modes of nuclear delivery. Third, endurance entailed the ability for a prolonged postattack endurance, so that a US retaliatory response could be carefully measured.[45]

Initially, engineers designed the Atlas to operate above ground, in the open, with only early warning and dispersion of launchers as survivability countermeasures. In a letter to General Power (CINCSAC), Gen Thomas D. White outlined the operational requirements for fielding the Atlas—each missile site needed to be able to launch 10 missiles within 15 minutes after an alert warning and an additional 10 missiles within the next two hours.[46] Recognizing the vulnerability of the exposed Atlas missile, engineers developed further survivability measures. The USAF placed the Atlas missile within a "semi-hardened" horizontal silo called the "coffin" and advocated a 3 x 3 dispersed configuration. The 3 x 3 configuration entailed three complexes of three launchers per complex. ICBM basing plans required a minimum of 18 miles dispersion between complexes. Upon launch order, a hydraulic lift would place the Atlas missile in the vertical position ready for activation. Further studies on this system revealed limited survivability, high cost of maintenance of elevators, and slower-than-desired reaction times to launch.[47]

Additional studies continued, specifically examining alternative approaches for ICBM employment, such as optimal missile-base design, site-selection criteria, and cost requirements. Ultimately, on 20 December 1955, Generals LeMay and Power decided on ICBM site requirements. Due to an urgent desire to operationally field an ICBM, the initial sites would be above ground. However, subsequent missile sites required hardened, underground silos and vertically stored missiles ready for immediate launching.[48] Therefore, the operational fielding of the Atlas would permit aboveground sites, but the Titan and Minuteman would require hardened, underground silos.

On 4 October 1957, the successful Soviet launching of Sputnik aggravated fears of Soviet technological superiority (a "missile gap") and spurred further acceleration of US ICBM development. The Sputnik launch proved fortuitous for the Titan program, as it was beginning to languish from budgetary neglect. Across the board, USAF leaders demanded rigorous operational readiness schedules and emphasized ICBM survival through underground hardening, dispersal, and mobility.[49] The USAF's development of the Titan was crucial to enhancing the survivability of ICBMs. Survivability requirements for the Titan drove the creation of hardened, underground silos capable of withstanding 300 pounds per square inch of overpressure. The Titan went to a 1 x 9 dispersal configuration and eliminated the need for an elevator by firing directly from a vertical position within the silo.[50] These actions enhanced the survivability and quick reaction time of the Titan system.

The next step for the United States in increasing the survivability of its missile force was to address mobility. In 1960, the US Navy successfully launched a Polaris missile from a submarine, ushering in a third aspect of the strategic nuclear triad, submarine-launched ballistic missiles. Thus, by the time solid-fueled Minuteman missiles became operational during the Cuban missile crisis in October 1962, the United States had developed its strategic nuclear forces from a purely air-based operation to a more survivable triad. The United States created a strategic triad that was capable of surviving any enemy aggression, could provide a diversity of responses, and was coercive in its perceived threat. Once again, the lessons learned from fielding ICBM units directly apply toward answering the antiaccess challenge in the Pacific Rim. Underground hardening, dispersal, mobility, alert procedures, and early warning systems are all pertinent aspects in increasing the survivability and sustainability of US overseas bases.

Summary of Lessons Learned

In response to the growing Soviet atomic weapons threat, SAC implemented the Reflex Action operational concept, and the United States fielded a strategic triad. Both actions offer significant insights toward improving current and future operational concepts to answer the antiaccess challenge in the Pacific Rim. As in the previous chapter, lessons learned were divided into strategic, operational, and tactical categories.

Several significant strategic-level lessons emerged from US actions to expand the viability of its strategic triad in the 1950s and early 1960s, which apply directly to the emerging antiaccess threat in the Pacific Rim. Many of these reinforce those lessons learned by USAFE as described in chapter 3. Briefly, these strategic lessons are: (1) the importance of linking the development of military capability to the grand strategy; (2) understanding the relationship between military capability and strategic-coercion theory; (3) how future military capabilities address US vulnerabilities and counter potential enemy strategies; and (4) how US force posture and operational concepts expand US options and shrink those of potential adversaries.[51] More specifically, any Pacific Rim operational concept must consider three key facets of grand strategy: (1) the deterrence of weapons of mass destruction; (2) the ability to communicate intent as clearly as possible; and (3) the clear conveyance of credibility and commitment. The US development of the strategic triad enhanced the survivability and operational capability of its combat assets by increasing the options the military could use to conduct combat operations. By addressing the vulnerability and capability of its combat assets, the military directly increased its own power-projection capability and the political viability of US foreign policy.

A Pacific Rim concept of operations needs to embrace several important operational elements: alert and responsive, combat effective, dispersed, expeditionary and forward deployed, survivable, and sustainable. A Pacific Rim framework must integrate these elements to optimize combat capability in a geographically demanding region. The multiple benefits from integrating these elements into an operational concept are as follows: demonstrate US credibility in regard to fighting within threat rings; demonstrate the willingness to accept risks similar to its allies; signal US intentions toward adversaries; increase the endurance and persistence of US involvement; enhance US ability to measure and control the degree of escalation; and shape an adversary's response. These operational advantages also accrue to the strategic and diplomatic levels.

During the 1950s and early 1960s, US actions toward enhancing and building its strategic triad generated valuable operational lessons directly applicable to the Pacific Rim. First, an effective framework was developed for conducting strategic operations. The framework supplied several important capabilities for military operations, such as expeditionary mobility and sustainability, dispersed operations, maintenance of an alert posture for extended periods, and hardened survivability of bases. All of these capabilities are important in developing an effective operational concept specifically designed for the Pacific Rim antiaccess challenge. Second, SAC recognized the importance of rotating all units through dispersed locations on a continual cycle. The expeditionary mind-set is crucial for today's Air Force, which is heavily tasked to meet global challenges. Third, a balanced force structure and dispersed operations make an adversary's strategy-building and targeting increasingly complex. Within the Pacific Rim, all US military forces need to collectively provide a balanced approach to conducting combat operations. If the USAF increases its basing options in the Pacific, potential adversaries will face a more difficult challenge in access denial. Overall sustainability and survivability would increase for all US military services. Fourth, the need for tanker operations as a critical force enhancer requires careful consideration by planners. Tanker deployments, although critical, are less coercive and therefore more palatable to US allies in the Pacific Rim. Fifth, desired capabilities must drive future weapon systems procurement and the development of operational concepts.

The US "crash course" in missile procurement provided several vital tactical-level lessons learned directly applicable to the Pacific Rim. Most importantly, survivability and sustainability of an operational concept or weapon system require addressing vulnerabilities. In the Pacific Rim, fixed bases present several vulnerabilities that need to be addressed. These include force protection, passive and active defense measures, sustainable logistics, and command, control, and communications.

The US efforts in the 1950s and early 1960s to enhance the survivability and operational combat effectiveness of its strategic triad provide important lessons in building any future operational concepts to counter growing antiaccess capabilities. The next chapter provides an operational concept that incorporates the lessons learned by the US military in the 1950s and 1960s to overcome the growing antiaccess challenge in the Pacific Rim, thereby increasing overall US combat effectiveness.

Notes

1. Fred Kaplan, *The Wizards of Armageddon* (New York: Simon and Schuster, 1983), 86.
2. Paul S. Killingsworth et al., *Flexbasing: Achieving Global Presence for Expeditionary Aerospace Forces*, RAND Report MR-1113-AF (Santa Monica, CA: RAND, 2000), 2.
3. Futrell, *Volume I*, 288.
4. Ibid., 289.
5. Killingsworth, *Flexbasing*, 93.
6. Kaplan, *Wizards of Armageddon*, 93–94.
7. Ibid., 99.
8. Ibid., 100.
9. Kaplan, *Wizards of Armageddon*, 106–7.

10. Alfred Wohlstetter and Fred Hoffman, *Defending a Strategic Force after 1960*, RAND Report D-2270 (Santa Monica, CA: RAND, 1 February 1954), 3.

11. Ibid., 1.

12. Ibid., 6–7.

13. Futrell, *Volume I*, 512.

14. Ibid.

15. Ibid., 513.

16. Killingsworth et. al, *Flexbasing*, 3. Additionally, it should be understood that although the SAC plan withdrew the bomber force to CONUS, the nuclear strike plan depended on theater bases throughout the Cold War.

17. Maj Gen J. V. Edmundson (DO) to Gen Thomas Power, memorandum, 25 July 1958, subj: "CINC Items on Northwest Trip," in *History of Strategic Air Command: June 1958–July 1959, Historical Study No. 76, Volume VIII* [Hereafter: *Historical Study 76/VIII*].

18. Maj Gen J. McConnell to Gen Thomas D. White, chief of staff, USAF, memorandum, 4 October 1957, subj: "SAC Rotational Forces," in *Historical Study 76/VIII*.

19. Headquarters Strategic Air Command, *The SAC Alert Program, 1956–1959, Historical Study No. 79, Volume I* (Offutt AFB, NE: SAC, 1960).

20. History, 305th MBW, 1 June–31 July 1957, 29.

21. See Memo for Record, "Report of TDY to Sidi Slimane," no date, HQ 2AF, July–December 1957, in *Historical Study 76/VIII*.

22. History, 3906th ABGp, July–December 1957, in *Historical Study 76/VIII*, 5–6.

23. *SAC Study No. 79*, 46.

24. Maj Gen J. D. Ryan to CINCSAC, memorandum, 7 November 1957, subj: "Overseas Staff Visit, 23 Oct–1 Nov 57," in *Historical Study 76/VIII*.

25. History, 305th MBW, November 1957.

26. History, 306th BW, August 1957.

27. Edgar O. Berdahl, HQ 2AF, memorandum for record, subj: "Comments on Reflex Action Based on Visit to Sidi Slimane, 23–27 Aug 57," in History, 2AF, July–December 1957.

28. Brig Gen K. K. Compton, commander 5AD, to Maj Gen G. W. Mundy (commander 2AF), letter, 1 October 1957, in *History of SAC, Jan–Jun 58, Chapter II, Volume III*.

29. Col Richard E. Barton, deputy chief of SAC DOOP, to SAC DOPL, memorandum, 19 December 1957, subj: "Alert Force Evaluation," in *History of SAC, Jan–Jun 58, Chapter II, Volume III*.

30. Maj Gen R. H. Terrill, SAC DO, Report: "Overseas Staff Visit, 27 Sep–12 Oct 57," in *Historical Study 76/VIII*.

31. "Operation Reflex Action," SAC memorandum, 12 June 1958, in *History of SAC, Jan–Jun 58, Chapter II, Volume III*.

32. Ibid.

33. Col W. M. Shy, deputy chief, Programs Division, SAC, memorandum, 19 December 1958, subj: "Review of SAC History," in *Historical Study 76/VIII*.

34. "Operation Reflex Action," 12 June 1958.

35. *SAC Study No. 79*, 54.

36. Maj Gen J. V. Edmundson, SAC DO, to Gen Thomas Power, memorandum, 25 July 1958, subj: "CINC Items on Northwest Trip," in *Historical Study 76/VIII*.

37. History, 3909th ABGp, May 1958, 11.

38. "SAC Air Operations Schedule (Peacetime)," 1 May 1958; and changes 1–4, in *Historical Study 76/VIII*.

39. Ibid.

40. *SAC Study No. 79*, 134.

41. Ibid., 135–36.

42. Futrell, *Volume I*, 489.

43. Ibid., 490.

44. Jacob Neufeld, *Ballistic Missiles in the United States Air Force, 1945–1960* (Washington, DC: Office of Air Force History, 1990), 3. The US services attempted to create an IRBM

capability concurrently. The USAF developed the Thor, while the USA and USN jointly developed the Jupiter until the USN broke off to develop its own Polaris missile.

45. Office of the Deputy Undersecretary of Defense, *ICBM Basing Options: A Summary of Major Studies to Define a Survivable Basing Concept for ICBMs* (Washington, DC: Office of the Deputy Undersecretary of Defense for Research and Engineering, December 1980), 4.

46. Neufeld, *Ballistic Missiles*, 121.

47. Ibid., 187, 193.

48. Ibid., 177.

49. Ibid., 190.

50. The 1 x 9 configuration meant that each missile was separately controlled and allowed for greater dispersal distances between launch sites.

51. For an excellent presentation on coercion theory, read Daniel Byman and Matthew Waxman, *The Dynamics of Coercion* (New York: Cambridge University Press, 2002).

Chapter 5

Answering the Antiaccess
Challenge in the Pacific Rim
An Operational Concept Proposal

[O]ur traditional access to forward bases . . . will likely decline precipitously over time. . . . This will ultimately require some major changes in existing operational concepts—and perhaps the emergence of new operational concepts—such as those designed to defeat the anti-access problem.

—Dr. Andrew Krepinevich, 1999

The antiaccess issue presents one of the greatest challenges to a bedrock US national security capability—power projection. Although many commentators, even many in the Pentagon, are just discovering this issue, the foregoing analysis shows the problem has significant and analytically important historic precedents. Moreover, power projection includes the ability to penetrate a region with diplomatic, economic, military, and informational means. Although this study focuses primarily on military access, it links any military operational concepts to the overarching US grand strategy. The operational concept proposed in this study is designed to expand US strategic options in the Pacific Rim, even as it addresses requirements down to the tactical level. Several elements of the overall proposal are important at the national policy level of debate.

Chapter 2 argues that the United States needs to focus on the Pacific Rim as its number one regional priority and should gradually shift its diplomatic and political resources away from Europe and the Middle East toward the Pacific Rim. Despite the immediacy of events in the Middle East, the Pacific Rim will emerge over the next 20 years as the global center of gravity for world affairs. A reallocation of cumulative capital to the Pacific Rim would allow the United States to position itself advantageously in this region. In the 2002 *National Security Strategy*, Pres. George W. Bush recognized the significance of strengthening relations with nations in the Pacific Rim, specifically, China, India, Russia, Japan, South Korea, and Australia.[1] The United States should ascertain and accomplish the efforts required to achieve a position of advantage for future opportunities in the Pacific Rim. If it implements a visionary Pacific Rim strategy, then it will reap the benefits of addressing challenges from a position of strength. In sum, the United States needs to lay the groundwork now in order to optimize its international diplomatic leverage in the future.

Access to overseas bases directly impacts the United States' ability to conduct effective diplomacy. The United States is well positioned geographically to enhance the stability of the Pacific Rim. Noted international relations theorist Stephen M. Walt described this best when he said:

> For the medium powers of Western Europe and Asia, the US is the perfect ally. It is sufficiently powerful to contribute substantially to their defense, it is driven by its own concerns to oppose Soviet expansion, and yet it is sufficiently distant from those allies so it does not itself pose a significant threat. Thus, the United States is geographically isolated but politically popular, while the Soviet Union is politically isolated as a consequence of geographic proximity. More than any other factor, geography explains why so many of the world's significant powers have chosen to ally with the US.[2]

Although the Soviet Union is no more, the same principle would apply if another nation exercised hegemonic aspirations in the Pacific Rim. Similarly, authors Thomas C. Schelling and Robert E. Harkavy add further weight to the importance of overseas bases and access in international relations.

On a fundamental level, Schelling recognized the overarching importance of controlling or manipulating options. In international relations, the answer is not just to have the most options, but also to control any options available to the adversary. According to Schelling, US overseas coercion depends on a complex process of manipulating options.[3] In the Pacific Rim, a network of land-based airfields will facilitate the United States' ability to control options. US national leadership can choose from a menu of measured responses for a multitude of contingencies, from humanitarian assistance to direct conflict. Land bases provide distinct advantages that complement other (e.g., naval) US power-projection means, but in light of the advancing threat in the region, the United States has an underdeveloped land-based infrastructure.

Specifically, Harkavy identified the importance of overseas basing in international relations during the tense Cold War standoff between the United States and the Soviet Union. According to Harkavy,

> On both sides, the availability—or its lack of—overseas bases was to play a crucial role in calculations about the nuclear balance, mutual deterrence, and fears of first-strike vulnerability. Foreign access was to play a role both for offensive and defensive systems in this context, as well as for crucial intelligence monitoring capability and for related communications. . . . The balance of advantage was all on the American side, given the extensive U.S. ring of bases around the USSR and the latter's complete lack of equivalent access.[4]

After World War II, the United States maintained an extensive set of basing options throughout Europe and the Pacific. However, with the end of the Cold War, it has dramatically reduced its force structure, both in bases and manpower. Therefore, the United States needs to selectively choose how and where to allocate its finite military resources in the future for optimal benefit.

Currently, US overseas basing in the Pacific Rim, located predominantly in the northeast section, is inadequate to meet the future requirements of the region. An enormous geographic coverage gap exists between Guam in the Pacific Ocean and Diego Garcia in the Indian Ocean. The US basing posture is inadequate to respond rapidly and persistently to crises occurring in this gap. Furthermore, these bases and the resources situated therein are of limited utility. It is possible that in the event of a conflict with

China, many bases located in South Korea and Japan may prove diplomatically unusable. If these bases are subtracted through diplomatic antiaccess actions, US power-projection capability and sustainability become tenuous. This would force an overreliance on the Navy's carrier force, which has severe sustainability issues and already faces an increasing antiaccess challenge of its own. Therefore, the United States must develop a more comprehensive basing framework in the Pacific Rim to enhance and complement its naval power-projection capability. The following proposal provides a recommended answer to the growing antiaccess challenge in the Pacific Rim.

USAFE's dispersal program of the late 1950s provides a substantial foundation from which to address US access needs in the Pacific Rim. Similar to the USAFE system of main operating bases, dispersed operating bases, and dispersed landing bases, in this proposal the United States will build and implement a three-tiered basing network. The Tier 1 bases will be US controlled and will contain a full complement of air assets—approximately three squadrons (50–70 aircraft). These bases will include all the necessary logistics to supply and maintain combat operations for extended periods of time. US personnel will operate year-round at Tier 1 bases.

Tier 2 bases will be dispersal airfields with sufficient infrastructure to support combat operations. They will offer forward deployment and dispersal of individual squadrons and will include sufficient logistics to allow limited maintenance operations, fuel, and munitions supplies for approximately 30 days' operations. Tier 2 airfields will belong to host nations, which will grant the United States access in times of coalition exercises or contingency operations. The United States will retain a small contingent of two to five operators at these airfields to facilitate use by US forces.

Finally, Tier 3 bases will provide further dispersal airfields, which allow limited dispersed operations or recovery for individual aircraft. They are austere airfields, sufficient only to launch or recover aircraft for a three-day period. Resupply considerations will require careful intra-theater planning. Host nations will retain control of these bases; US use will be contingent upon approval. US personnel will not be permanently located at these "bare" bases. Instead, Tier 2 personnel will monitor Tier 3 bases and ascertain their ability for use by US aircraft.

Host nation retention and maintenance of Tier 2 and Tier 3 bases is a critical component of the Pacific Rim dispersed operational concept. During the Cold War, European countries lived under the credible possibility that the Soviet Union could conquer Western Europe. The fear of conquest motivated Western European countries to allow US military access via a comprehensive network of bases, especially throughout West Germany. The United States permanently stationed military forces in Western Europe throughout the Cold War period. In contrast, the Pacific Rim does not currently face such a perceived expansionist adversary as the Soviet Union. Thus, the United States cannot leverage a substantial threat to national survivability to gain access across Asia with a network of permanent bases.

Instead, it must carefully develop diplomatic relations—sprinkled with military and economic incentives—with Asian nations to gain conditional access when required.

There is a threefold positive aspect to this contextual reality in the Pacific Rim. First, the United States will not incur the total cost required to build, maintain, or operate an enormous quantity of airfields in peacetime to guarantee access in wartime. Second, host-nation retention minimizes cultural tension between locals and substantial US military personnel permanently stationed in country. Third, the large quantity of US manpower required to operate these bases is eliminated. Fortunately, the Pacific Rim has sufficient airfields to support the proposed Tier 1, Tier 2, and Tier 3 basing construct. Conversely, the United States does not maintain an adequate basing structure within the Pacific Rim to cover the vast distances. See appendix for current Pacific Rim airfield locations and lengths.

The United States needs to dramatically increase its Pacific Rim basing structure to ensure its ability to conduct rapid, sustainable, survivable, and precise operations with decisive results; to provide a viable infrastructure from which antiterrorism operations can be staged; to accomplish joint and combined exercises within the region; and to assist in humanitarian efforts for emergency situations.[5] It should build Tier 1 bases in the Pacific Rim, forming a perimeter stretching from Diego Garcia in the Indian Ocean to Elmendorf AFB in Alaska. Intermediate basing locations could potentially include Darwin, Australia; Palau; Anderson AFB, Guam; Wake Island; and the Christmas Islands.[6] Optimally, six Tier 1 bases would form the core of this perimeter.

Tier 1 bases would provide multiple advantages: (1) a network of sustainable forward bases; (2) improved capability to safely pre-position large amounts of resources across an entire region; (3) enhanced overall survivability of joint forces due to a more balanced power-projection capability that increases the magnitude and complexity of an adversary's strategic challenge; (4) multiple staging areas for conducting air and naval operations; (5) a relatively safe haven for high-value airborne assets such as stealth bombers and Airborne Warning and Control Systems (AWACS); (6) the infrastructure to support forward-located combined air operations centers (CAOC) and major depot centers for supplies and parts; (7) more survivable dispersed operations that present multiple avenues of penetration into adversary airspace; and (8) greater security for operations than current base structure offers by presenting more but smaller targets for enemy action.[7]

The United States needs to carefully select the locations of Tier 1 bases. Due to their significance for political and operational strategies, these relatively large bases should only be developed at locations under direct US control, or in conjunction with time-proven, reliable allies. There is also the need to balance the risk scale between vulnerability and distance. The crux of this dilemma is the vulnerability of land bases to the threat of emerging precision-capable ballistic missiles versus the operational requirement to forward deploy power-projection assets for persistent, sustainable firepower against an adversary. The sites advocated above attempt to balance the risk scale by placing the Tier 1 bases approximately 2,000 miles from potential threats, predominately the Chinese DF-21 missiles and Tu-16 bombers.[8] These bases will minimize the threat posed by antiaccess technological systems, while maximizing the US capability to conduct robust operations into the Pacific Rim.

The US response to Soviet ICBM development in the 1950s and 1960s offers valuable lessons for enhancing the survivability of fixed land bases in the Pacific Rim. Tier 1 bases will require base-survivability and force-protection characteristics. First, they need to be hardened to the maximum extent possible and have hardened shelters sufficient to house approximately three squadrons (50+ aircraft). Second, they need hardened, dispersed, underground facilities for critical resources such as fuel, munitions, and command, control, and communications. Third, base survivability should be enhanced with theater missile-defense systems and GPS jammers. Fourth, the bases must be designed to maximize passive defense systems such as dispersal of assets, reinforced revetments, and camouflage or other deception measures. Fifth, Tier 1 bases will require permanent manning by US military personnel, similar to Anderson AFB, Guam, where US personnel continually maintain base operations. The United States should augment the manning and exercise the use of Tier 1 bases with rotational forces associated with AEFs. During peacetime, the number of permanent assigned forces at Tier 1 bases should be kept to a minimum, while still guaranteeing base readiness for expansion in time of conflict. Collectively, these measures should create a perimeter of hardened bases capable of sustaining future US power-projection capabilities into the region. From this Tier 1 base foundation, further coverage and penetration of the Pacific Rim will occur with the Tier 2 dispersed basing plan.

A Tier 2 basing network must enable effective air operations within adversary missile threat rings. This recommendation is based on several assumptions. First, adversaries will continue to enhance their antiaccess capabilities by expanding the range and increasing the precision of missiles. As during the Cold War, missile threat rings will only expand and become more precise. In the 1950s, the requirement for European presence and shared risk necessitated aggressive new operational concepts, and the United States must be prepared to implement the same sort of measures in the Pacific Rim. Second, locating operating bases closer to the locus of conflict increases the combat potential of US forces, even as it increases vulnerability. The acceptance of this risk versus reward signals to adversaries and allies important messages of commitment, credibility, and capability. Third, a more balanced, multidimensional power-projection structure in the Pacific Rim strengthens the United States diplomatically and presents a much more difficult strategic problem to adversaries. Currently, the joint force structure is out of balance in the region. There is an overreliance on carriers and a few large land bases. Specifically, USAF bases are not distributed widely enough across the Pacific Rim to provide sufficient coverage for this immense region, thus causing an unbalanced reliance on either long-range bombers or force extension through tankers. Therefore, if the United States were to balance the initial strike burden between forces based in-theater, such as carriers and tactical air forces, and forces based outside the region, such as long-range bombers, overall combat effectiveness and deterrent potential would increase.[9] Fourth, the United States still requires an enabling force in-theater to provide at least the following capabilities: air superiority to defend key assets from enemy fighter attack; suppression of enemy air defenses; and strike forces with sustained sortie-generation capability. Fifth, it must make the in-theater bases and aircraft survivable in order to enable a sustained campaign.[10] The United States should develop mobile protection packages of passive and active defense measures, pre-position them at Tier 1 bases, and then send them forward to the selected Tier 2 base upon initiation of conflict.

The United States could face an adversary with significant antiaccess capability. The potential threat environment, in this case, would include WMD, precision conventional ballistic and cruise missiles, and advanced aircraft. In sum, the political and military advantages attained from forward deploying in-theater outweigh the risks of exposure to adversarial antiaccess measures. Based on this equation, the United States requires a dispersed operational concept in support of the Global Strike concept of operations.

Selection of Tier 2 bases will demand dispersed forward locations well within current antiaccess threat rings.[11] According to Christopher Bowie, USAF procurement plans indicate that for the next three decades, for conflicts of any significant size, it will require secure access to sufficient bases within 1,000 to 1,500 nautical miles of the theater of conflict to project power against an adversary equipped with modern air defense systems.[12]

New weapon systems, such as the F-22 joint strike fighter and the unmanned combat aerial vehicle (UCAV), necessitate in-theater basing requirements to achieve persistence, sortie generation, and loiter time necessary to project power at rates and efficiencies not attainable by long-range systems. Like the USAFE dispersal program (chap. 3), the Pacific Rim dispersed operational concept requires the capability of AEFs to deploy not only on a rotational basis in peacetime, but also to deploy rapidly to dispersed bases during times of rising tensions in-theater. During a crisis, units within an AEF would disperse to Tier 2 bases, remaining networked to the Tier 1 bases for logistics and control. Operational, command and control, and logistical requirements would determine the optimum separation distances between Tier 1 and Tier 2 bases. The separation would provide enhanced protection for the Tier 1 and Tier 2 bases to survive antiaccess missile and bomber attacks in the aggregate. Additionally, further dispersal of assets forward deployed to Tier 2 bases would provide greater survivability against threats in-theater.

The USAFE dispersal program provides valuable insights for enhancing the survivability of fixed land bases in the Pacific Rim within a future dispersed operational concept. As exercised by USAFE in the 1950s, the Pacific Rim dispersed operational concept would require each Tier 2 base to have multiple Tier 3 dispersal bases. The Tier 2 base would function as the primary operating base for the assigned AEF units, while the Tier 3 bases would function as secondary dispersal locations. The Pacific Rim dispersed operational concept would improve the operational balance of forces in the Pacific Rim and generate several advantages: (1) upgraded force protection of US military forces in-theater due to greater survivability through dispersion; (2) increased targeting difficulties for a potential adversary; and (3) a signal to allies and enemies of a willingness to operate under adverse antiaccess conditions. Infrastructure requirements for Tier 2 and Tier 3 bases are less than those required for Tier 1 bases. There is a spectrum of airfields sufficient to conduct effective Tier 2 base operations in the Pacific Rim, including more than 650 with runways greater than 6,000 feet within 2,000 miles of Taiwan. The spectrum ranges from currently developed airfields already hosting US forces—such as Kadena AB, Japan—to bare, host-nation airfields that need assistance to build infrastructure for conducting operations.

SAC's Reflex Action expeditionary operational concept for deploying its long-range bombers forward to counter the Soviet threat provides crucial insights for enhancing the survivability of future expeditionary operations at fixed land bases. SAC recognized the importance of maintaining overseas bases, especially to conduct combat operations capable of penetrating deep into Soviet territory. Due to the potential short warning of an incoming Soviet attack, SAC believed only those aircraft on an alert status could provide a sufficient retaliatory capability; therefore, it maintained only an alert force overseas. SAC based this decision on the necessity of attacking Soviet targets as soon as possible after initial warning; the limited number of tankers available to launch exclusively from CONUS bases; and the advantages of dispersed locations as they increased the difficulties of targeting for an attacker attempting a surprise attack. These access considerations remain true today in the Pacific Rim. Therefore, when the United States is required to conduct combat operations from Tier 2 bases, its forces will retain an alert posture with aircraft in ready-to-launch status.

All Tier 2 bases need sufficient survivability and sustainability to operate long enough to suppress modern enemy air defenses. This requires several important conditions. First, the Tier 2 bases would remain under the sovereign host nation's control and will only become operational during expeditionary exercises and emergency crises. The host nation would operate and maintain the bases for their own uses in the interim. The United States will develop and maintain a corps of airfield-management experts with the required linguistic and cultural training to act as airfield liaisons. They would be permanently located in-theater and would oversee the maintenance of several Tier 2 and Tier 3 airfields, making sure the airfields remain prepared for future operations. The airfield liaisons would coordinate US efforts to use these airfields with local host governments.[13]

It is not cost effective for the United States to build sufficient bases across the Pacific Rim to guarantee access during times of crisis, so it must therefore rely on other measures to ensure access to Tier 2 bases when needed. The United States could create monetary incentives to encourage Pacific Rim nations to build sufficient bases, grant US access, and develop airfields capable of supporting combat operations. Nations willing to allow US forces to operate from their airfields would receive improved facilities and equipment. Additionally, the United States could conduct cooperative military exercises to enhance coalition and host-nation military capabilities from these airfields. Upon gaining access during conflict, the United States would offer to move active and passive force-protection measures to the Tier 2 bases, which would diminish fear of attack. If possible or secure enough, the United States should attempt to pre-position approximately two weeks' operational supplies at the Tier 2 bases. Tier 3 bases are austere airfields capable only of launching and recovering aircraft during conflicts that require dispersal operations.

The Tier 2 and Tier 3 basing arrangement offers several advantages. First, it minimizes the costs of maintaining a large airfield network. The opportunity to exercise these airfields during peacetime with host-nation participation would improve US expeditionary capability, host-nation military capability, and the interoperability between the United States and the host nation while the host nation incurs the cost of operating the airfield on a continual basis. Second, US personnel requirements are small; the only permanently located US personnel would be the airfield-management liaisons. The United States should use these airfields to conduct periodic operational exercises. Third, it is a valuable diplomatic coercion tool. The United States can use Tier 2 airfields for signaling intentions to an adversary during an emerging crisis. Potentially, it could flex the Pacific Rim dispersed operational concept under the auspices of a training exercise, a site survey, or a humanitarian assistance operation to convey US commitment. Fourth, the USAF could exercise its expeditionary combat capability. The Pacific Rim dispersed operational concept offers the opportunity to exercise US forces in expeditionary operations to minimal standard bases. Rather than cycling AEF rotations through established airfields, the USAF could continue to train subsequent generations of airmen in expeditionary operations at bare bases. In coordination with host nations, an AEF cycle could begin with advanced logistics teams preparing an airfield for the arrival of operational units. Operational units could process through Tier 1 bases or proceed directly to Tier 2 bases when ready. Fifth, US forces could effectively incorporate joint training and operations into the Pacific Rim dispersed operational concept. Exercising in expeditionary operations into austere, dispersed airfields will severely test a joint exercise's ability to plan, coordinate, communicate, command, control, and execute.[14] Finally, a network of Tier 1, Tier 2, and Tier 3 bases offers much-needed additional coverage of the entire Pacific Rim. Currently, the United States relies on carrier battle groups for power projection into many parts of the Pacific.[15] A comprehensive Pacific Rim dispersed operational concept offers diverse power-projection capability and additional options for US policy makers. Similarly, a network of land bases generates a more balanced US force structure, better prepared for operations across the Pacific Rim at a moment's notice.[16]

Notes

1. *The National Security Strategy of the United States of America* (Washington, DC: The White House, September 2002), 26.

2. Stephen M. Walt, "Alliance Formation and the Balance of Power," in *The Perils of Anarchy: Contemporary Realism and International Security,* ed. Michael E. Brown et al. (Cambridge, MA: MIT Press, 1995), 241.

3. Thomas C. Schelling, *Arms and Influence* (New Haven, CT: Yale University Press, 1966), 44.

4. Robert E. Harkavy, *Great Power Competition for Overseas Bases: The Geopolitics of Access Diplomacy* (New York: Pergamon Press, 1982), 116.

5. The principle of continuously analyzing the current disposition of forces to make appropriate changes in the future is ancient. Sun Tzu stated, "Now the army's disposition of force is like water. Water's configuration avoids heights and races downward. The army's disposition of force avoids the substantial and strikes the vacuous. Water configures its flow in accord with the terrain; the army controls its victory in accord with the enemy. Thus, the enemy does not maintain any constant strategic configuration of power, water has no constant shape. One who is able to change and transform in accord with the enemy and wrest control is termed spiritual." Sun Tzu, *The Art of War* (San Francisco, CA: Westview Press, 1994), 193.

6. It is imperative that the United States gain guaranteed operational control and usage of Tier 1 bases during conflict due to the costs associated with building and maintaining these bases and the absolute demand for access when needed. Based on this requirement of guaranteed access, the building of Tier 1 bases is only recommended at locations where the United States has direct control or a historically staunch ally minimizes the risk of exclusion. Of particular note is Palau, a nation that ratified the Compact of Free Association with the United States on 1 October 1994. This compact provides Palau with up to $700 million in US aid over 15 years in return for furnishing military access and military facilities for 50 years.

7. The peril of overrelying on one main base or one avenue of attack as it creates an enormous center of gravity and potential vulnerability is given by J. C. Slessor. "The more aeroplanes there are concentrated on any one aerodrome the higher proportion of casualties are likely to result from air bombardment. This factor . . . really resolves itself into the question of the need for wider dispersion of aircraft on the ground." J. C. Slessor, *Air Power and Armies* (London: Oxford University Press, 1982), 57.

8. For a more complete discussion on China's military capability, read Frank W. Moore, "China's Military Capabilities" (Cambridge, MA: Institute for Defense and Disarmament Studies, June 2000).

9. Balancing US forces in the Pacific Rim allows for a more flexible force that still provides effective concentration. Naval theorist Sir Julian Corbett anticipated this effect when he wrote, "Concentration connotes not a homogeneous body, but a compound organism controlled from a common center, and elastic enough to permit it to cover a wide field without sacrificing the mutual support of its parts." Julian Corbett, *Some Principles of Maritime Strategy* (Annapolis, MD: Naval Institute Press, 1988), 131.

10. Future adversaries will recognize and desire to exploit Giulio Douhet's concept, "Destroying an enemy's airplanes by seeking them out in the air is, while not entirely useless, the least effective method. A much better way is to destroy his airports, supply bases and centers of production." Giulio Douhet, *The Command of the Air* (Washington, DC: Office of Air Force History, 1983), 34.

11. B. H. Liddell Hart offers some thoughts pertaining to the concept of dispersed operations and some of the tensions involved. Liddell Hart stated, "A revival of the distributed strategic advance was required in order to revive the art and effect of strategy. Moreover, new conditions—air-power and motor power—point to its further development into a dispersed strategic advance. The danger of air attack, the aim of mystification, and the need of drawing full value from mechanized mobility, suggest that advancing forces should not only be distributed as widely as is compatible with combined action, but be dispersed as much as is compatible with cohesion." B. H. Liddell Hart, *Strategy* (New York: Penguin Books, 1991), 332.

12. Christopher J. Bowie, *The Anti-Access Threat and Theater Air Bases* (Washington, DC: Center for Strategic and Budgetary Assessments, 2002), 15.

13. Andrew Marshall, interview by author, 4 December 2002.

14. The essence of exercising the concept of dispersed operations within joint training is distilled by Sir Julian Corbett. "The essential distinction of strategic deployment, which contemplates dispersal with a view to a choice of combinations, is flexibility and free movement. . . . In the one sense of concentration we contemplate a disposal of force which will conceal our intention from the enemy and will permit us to adapt our movements to the plan of operation he develops." Julian S. Corbett, *Some Principles of Maritime Strategy* (Annapoliis, MD: Naval Institute Press, 1980) 129–30.

15. The bottom line is best expressed by Gen Billy Mitchell, "Floating bases or aircraft carriers cannot compete with aircraft acting from land bases." William "Billy" Mitchell, *Winged Defense: The Development and Possibilities of Modern Air Power and Economic and Military* (Mineola, NY: Dover Publications, Inc., 1988), 102.

16. Underlying this concept is B. H. Liddell Hart's statement that, "Fluidity of force may succeed where concentration of force merely entails a perilous rigidity." B. H. Liddell Hart, *The Classic Book on Military Strategy* (New York: Penguin Books, 1991), 333.

Chapter 6

Conclusion

The cornerstone of America's continued military preeminence is our ability to project combat power rapidly and virtually unimpeded to widespread areas of the globe.

—National Defense Panel, 1997

Potential adversaries of the United States recognize that its ability to project combat power across the globe is essential to maintaining military dominance. Degrading US combat power projection requires a strategy of access denial which consists of geopolitical and military measures. In the Pacific Rim, development of antiaccess capabilities is accelerating. Specifically, China has increased its procurement of ballistic, cruise, and antiship missiles, sea mines, and diesel submarines with a special focus on anticarrier operations. Although China seems focused on naval forces, the antiaccess challenge affects all services.

Currently, the United States relies too heavily on naval forces in the Pacific Rim for power projection.* The overreliance on a single service creates vulnerabilities in the overall power projection capability. Since the Pacific Rim continues to emerge as a global region of importance, the United States must implement access-enhancing measures now to optimize its power-projection capability later. The central question for the Air Force centers on how land-based airpower can assist in answering the emerging antiaccess challenge in the Pacific Rim.

This is not the first time the United States has faced a significant antiaccess challenge. It encountered a severe challenge from the Soviet Union during the Cold War. In the 1950s and 1960s, the Soviets confronted the United States with nuclear delivery means (aircraft, IRBMs, and ICBMs) that threatened US military forces overseas and stateside. The United States answered this antiaccess challenge in a multifaceted approach that should inform our efforts in the Pacific Rim today. First, USAFE implemented dispersal plans for US tactical forces in Europe in response to the growing Soviet threat. The USAFE dispersal program addressed the inherent vulnerability of air assets at fixed locations by maximizing dispersal options and enhancing passive and active airfield defenses. Second, SAC put in place an operational concept called Reflex Action. Reflex Action enhanced the survivability of the long-range bomber force through dispersal and forward-deployed alert operations supported by an enhanced early

---

*Current US force structure relies heavily on permanent forward bases in the northern sectors of the Pacific Rim. In the middle and south sectors, the United States relies almost exclusively on naval force projection in the form of carrier battle groups and amphibious ready groups, both of which are the focus of Chinese antiaccess measures.

warning system. SAC retained a viable deterrent capability because Reflex Action enabled its long-range bombers to survive a surprise attack and mount a devastating counterattack. Third, the successful pursuit of a strategic triad—composed of long-range bombers, ICBMs and IRBMs, and sea-based SLBMs—allowed the United States to retain a strategic advantage throughout the Cold War. Similar to USAFE's dispersal plan, US nuclear planners employed multiple countermeasures to protect the fixed ICBM sites: underground hardening, dispersal, mobility, alert procedures, and early warning systems. Insights gained from implementing these measures to counter the Soviet threat apply directly as the United States deals with a growing Pacific Rim antiaccess challenge.

The Pacific Rim dispersed operational concept enhances the survivability and sustainability of US military forces against a robust and growing antiaccess threat by incorporating the most significant lessons derived from countering the Soviet threat during the Cold War. The three-tier system allows for maximum dispersion of air assets while retaining operational cohesion, even as it lends diplomatic strength to ties with nations in the region. The Pacific Rim dispersed operational concept provides the following advantages:

1. It focuses on ensuring US access into the Pacific Rim during periods of crisis without the expense of permanent bases.

2. It increases political and military options for US national leadership.

3. It requires less overall cost to the United States; host nations will incur the majority of operational costs for Tier 2 and Tier 3 bases as well as derive day-to-day utility from these bases.

4. It decreases cultural tension between the United States and host nations, as minimal US personnel are required to maintain Tier 2 and Tier 3 bases.

5. It enhances the United States' ability to conduct rapid, sustainable, survivable, and precise combat operations versus the present situation.

6. It provides a viable infrastructure from which the United States can conduct operations across the spectrum of war.

7. It augments the United States' ability to conduct joint and coalition operations in support of national objectives.

8. It provides a more balanced force structure within the Pacific Rim, which increases the survivability of US naval forces while increasing the magnitude and complexity of an adversary's strategic challenge.

9. It creates a network of bases capable of penetrating across the Pacific Rim from multiple axes of attack, diminishing the vulnerability associated with overreliance on too few bases in-theater.

10. It offers multiple hardened bases sufficient for locating CAOCs and logistical hubs.
11. It is congruent with current and evolving Air Force operational concepts, force structure, organizational constructs, and procurement systems.
12. It complements efforts by sister services to answer the anti-access challenge.
13. It incorporates in-theater tactical considerations and long-range bomber aspects.

The Pacific Rim dispersed operational concept enjoys significant advantages over current employment concepts; yet, several challenges will need to be addressed to implement it. First, the United States must carefully consider the support airlift requirements—inter- and intratheater—which may be substantial and possibly require addressing airlift and tanker force structures. Second, it must grant a higher degree of control to host nations of Tier 2 and Tier 3 bases. During times of crisis, the United States will need diplomacy to gain military access to these bases, similar to the current situation in the Middle East in which it leveraged basing and overflight access after the crisis emerged. Third, the initial costs are high for building the hardened infrastructure on Tier 1 bases. Fourth, this is a long-term strategic vision and requires substantial political vision and dedication to implement fully.

Policy Recommendations

Recognizing the initial costs associated with implementing this operational concept, the United States should begin building the hardened Tier 1 bases incrementally. The island nation of Palau offers an immediate, viable, and politically attractive option. Palau's location, 1,260 miles by air from Taipei, offers an attractive location for initiating the migration of bases toward the western and southern parts of the Pacific Rim. Conveniently, the United States signed an agreement with Palau in 1993 that allows for the development of military facilities and guarantees access for the next 50 years. In sum, the single most important near-term step the United States should consider implementing is the building of a Tier 1 base on Palau. Subsequently, it should continue to plan a network of bases stretching westward across the Pacific Rim, ultimately providing a Tier 1 perimeter from Elmendorf AFB, Alaska, to Diego Garcia in the Indian Ocean.

Areas for Further Study

Further research is required in several areas to enhance the viability of this concept: (1) the specific logistical requirements; (2) a detailed analysis of passive and active defenses that would maximize the survivability of land bases; (3) a detailed analysis of the requirements and costs of building hardened Tier 1 bases; (4) ways to integrate the dispersed operational concept within the AEF construct; and (5) selecting Tier 1 bases that would provide the most viable political and operational options.

The Pacific Rim dispersed operational concept complements the existing US force structure and is congruent with Air Force operational concepts and planned procurement programs. The operational concept supports integrated joint operations, the Air Force's Global Strike CONOPS, and the procurement of F/A-22, F-35A, and UCAV weapon systems. Additionally, the massive effort the United States is currently undertaking to integrate command, control, communications, computers, intelligence, surveillance, and reconnaissance, and the "global information grid" only enhance its capability to conduct dispersed operations and maintain an alert posture. Therefore, as Global Strike CONOPS attempts to fill the requirement for US forces to penetrate modern air defenses and knock down other key adversary antiaccess capabilities, the Pacific Rim dispersed operational concept attempts to answer the survivability and sustainability requirements of the land bases from which Global Strike CONOPS forces would launch. Furthermore, the Pacific Rim dispersed operational concept takes full advantage of the USAF's expeditionary nature and aligns perfectly with the current AEF construct. In fact, the genesis of this concept is rooted in the expeditionary efforts of SAC and USAFE to meet and defeat the Soviet antiaccess challenge. The Pacific Rim dispersed operational concept provides a comprehensive, survivable basing framework, which enables a balance of inter- and intratheater air assets in conjunction with joint and coalition forces to most effectively and efficiently achieve decisive results.

The Pacific Rim dispersed operational concept is a key enabler in continuing the US tradition of exploiting its asymmetric advantages. The United States must maintain the capability to exploit its advantages of airpower across the depth and breadth of any future theater of conflict. Consequently, the Air Force must continue to develop operational concepts, strengthen organizational constructs, exploit emerging technologies, and establish doctrine to guarantee the capability of land-based air forces to fight from inside and outside enemy threat rings. Long-range strikes from outside the threat ring will not suffice against a resilient and defiant adversary. US forces need to penetrate an adversary's territory in depth with persistent and substantial power. The United States must pursue CONOPS that allow an increase in the effects desired, while decreasing its vulnerabilities, even as its adversaries attempt to diminish that capability. The Pacific Rim dispersed operational concept answers the emerging antiaccess challenge and ensures America's indispensable asymmetric advantage—air dominance—in that vital and increasingly important region.

Appendix A

Pacific Rim airfields, 6,000–8,000 feet

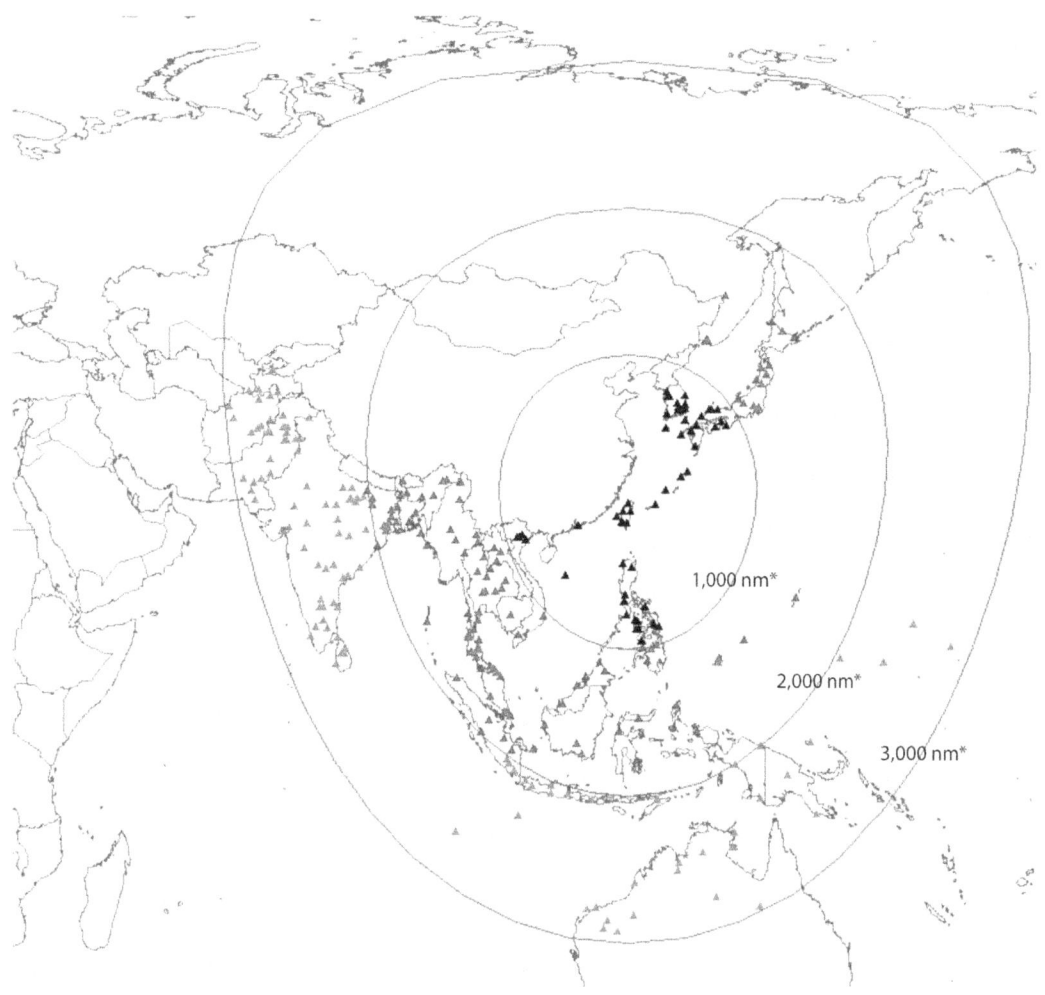

* Distance from Chiang Kai-Shek International Airport, Taiwan

Source: Pacific Air Forces Geographic Intelligence Office (PACAF GIO), June 2002.

Pacific Rim airfields, 8,000–10,000 feet

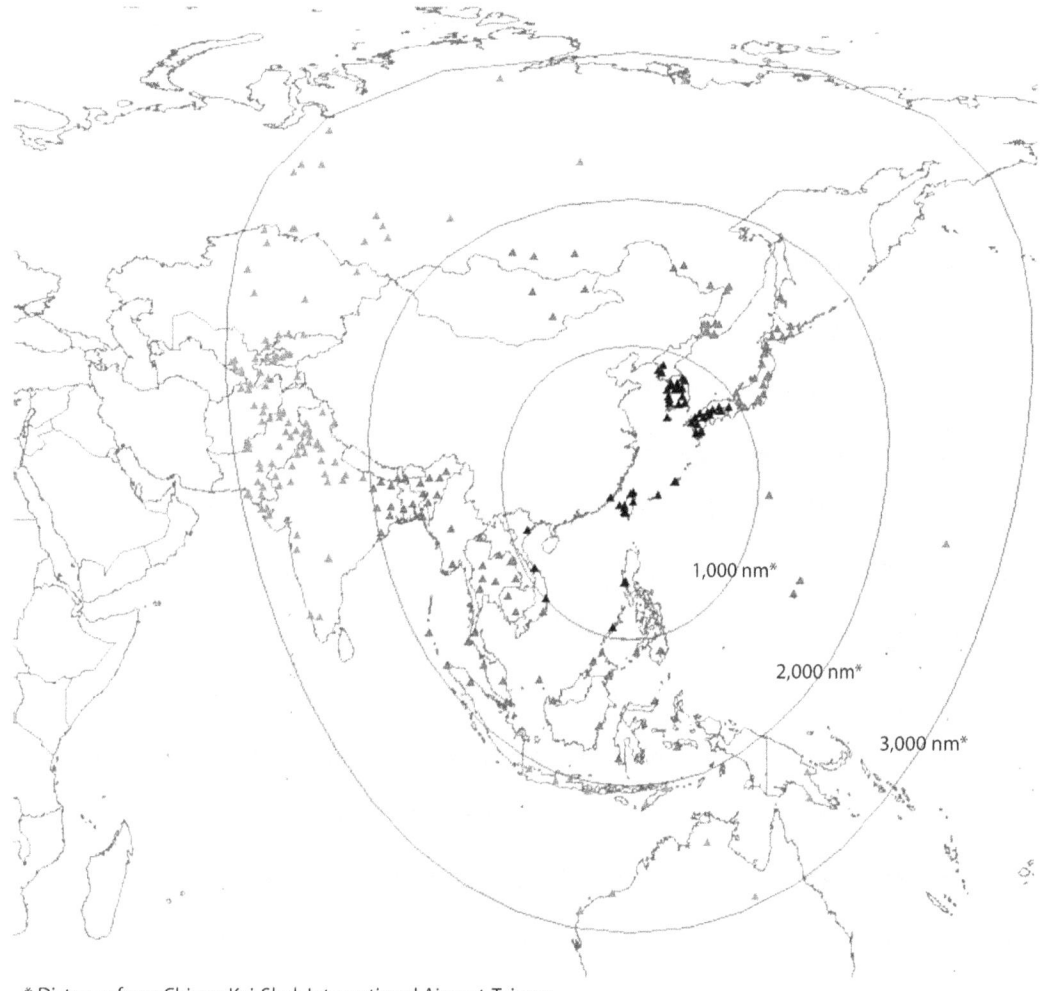

1,000 nm*

2,000 nm*

3,000 nm*

* Distance from Chiang Kai-Shek International Airport, Taiwan

Appendix C

Pacific Rim airfields, 10,000–12,000 feet

1,000 nm*

2,000 nm*

3,000 nm*

* Distance from Chiang Kai-Shek International Airport, Taiwan

Bibliography

Books

Allison, Graham, and Philip Zelikow. *Essence of Decision: Explaining the Cuban Missile Crisis.* New York: Addison-Wesley Educational Publishers, Inc., 1999.

Ball, Desmond. *Australia, the US Alliance, and Multilateralism in Southeast Asia.* Canberra, Australia: Australian National University, 1997.

Bertram, Christopher. *New Conventional Weapons and East-West Security.* New York: Praeger Publishers, 1979.

Bowie, Christopher J. *The Anti-Access Threat and Theater Air Bases.* Washington, DC: Center for Strategic and Budgetary Assessments, 2002.

Brands, H. W., Jr. *Cold Warriors: Eisenhower's Generation and American Foreign Policy.* New York: Columbia Press, 1988.

Byman, Daniel, and Matthew Waxman. *The Dynamics of Coercion.* New York: Cambridge University Press, 2002.

Byman, Daniel, Matthew Waxman, and Eric Larson. *Airpower as a Coercive Instrument.* MR-1061-AF. Santa Monica, CA: RAND Corp., 1999.

Center for Strategic and Budgetary Assessments. *Grand Strategy in Historical Perspective and Potential U.S.–China Competition.* Washington, DC: Center for Strategic and Budgetary Assessments (CSBA), 2001.

Cliff, Roger. *The Military Potentials of China's Commercial Technology.* RAND Corp., MR-1292-AF, 2001.

Corbett, Julian S. *Some Principles of Maritime Strategy.* Annapolis, MD: Naval Institute Press, 1988.

Coté, Owen R., Jr. *Assuring Access and Projecting Power: The Navy in the New Security Environment.* Cambridge, MA: MIT Security Studies Program, 2001.

———. "Buying '. . . From the Sea:' A Defense Budget for a Maritime Strategy." In *Holding the Line: U.S. Defense Alternatives for the Early 21st Century,* edited by Cindy Williams. Cambridge, MA: MIT Press, 2001.

Defense Science Board. *Final Report of the Defense Science Board Task Force on Globalization and Security.* Washington, DC: Office of the Undersecretary of Defense for Acquisition and Technology, December 1999.

Dolman, Everett C. *Astropolitik: Classical Geopolitics in the Space Age.* London: Frank Cass Publishers, 2002.

Douglass, Joseph D., Jr., and Amoretta M. Hoeber. *Soviet Strategy for Nuclear War.* Stanford, CA: Hoover Institution Press, 1979.

Douhet, Giulio. *The Command of the Air.* Salem, NH: Ayers Company Publishers, Inc., 1984.

Finletter, Thomas K. *Power and Policy: US Foreign Policy and Military Power in the Hydrogen Age.* New York: Harcourt, Brace and Co., 1954.

Futrell, Robert F. *Volume I Ideas, Concepts, Doctrine: Basic Thinking in the United States Air Force, 1907–1960.* Maxwell AFB, AL: Air University Press, December 1989.

Gaddis, John Lewis. *We Now Know: Rethinking Cold War History.* Oxford, UK: Clarendon Press, 1997.

George, Alexander L., and William E. Simons, eds. *The Limits of Coercive Diplomacy.* Boulder, CO: Westview, 1994.

Harkavy, Robert E. *Bases Abroad: The Global Foreign Military Presence.* New York: Oxford University Press, 1989.

———. *Great Power Competition for Overseas Bases: The Geopolitics of Access Diplomacy.* New York: Pergamon Press, 1982.

Holley, Irving B., Jr. "The Evolution of Operations Research and Its Impact on the Military Establishment; The Air Force Experience." In *Science, Technology, and Warfare: Proceedings of the Third Military History Symposium, United States Air Force Academy, 8–9 May 1969,* edited by Monte D. Wright and Lawrence J. Paszek. Washington, DC: Office of Air Force History and Air Force Academy, 1970.

Hoopes, Townsend. *The Devil and John Foster Dulles.* Boston: Atlantic Monthly Press Book, 1973.

Huntington, Samuel P. *The Common Defense: Strategic Programs in National Politics.* New York: Columbia University Press, 1961.

Ismay, Lord Hastings L. *NATO: The First Five Years, 1949–1954.* New York: Acme Cole Company, Inc., 1955.

Jain, J. P. *Documentary Study of the Warsaw Pact.* New York: Asia Publishing House, 1973.

Kagan, Korina. "The Failure of the Great Powers to Coerce Small States in the Balkans, 1875–1877 and 1914: Situational Versus Tactical Explanations." In *Strategic Coercion,* edited by Lawrence Freedman. New York: Oxford University Press, 1998.

Kaplan, Fred. *The Wizards of Armageddon.* New York: Simon and Schuster, 1983.

Kaplan, Morton A. *NATO & Dissuasion.* Chicago, IL: University of Chicago Press, 1974.

Khalilzad, Zalmay, J. D. Pollack, K. L. Pollpeter, A. Rabasa, and D. A. Schlapak. *The United States and Asia.* RAND Corp., MR-1315, 2001.

———. *The United States and a Rising China.* RAND Corp., MR-1082-AF, 1999.

Killingsworth, Paul, Lionel Galway, Eiichi Kamiya, Brian Nichiporak, Timothy L. Ramey, and Robert S. Tripp. *Flexbasing: Achieving Global Presence for Expeditionary Air Forces.* RAND Corp., MR-1113-AF, 2000.

Kolkowicz, Roman. *The Warsaw Pact: Report on a Conference on the Warsaw Treaty Organization Held at the Institute for Defense Analysis, May 17–19, 1967.* Arlington, VA: Institute for Defense Analysis, 1969.

Kwiatkowski, Lt Col Karen U. *Expeditionary Air Operations in Africa: Challenges and Solutions.* Maxwell AFB, AL: Air University Press, 2001.

Lewis, William J. *The Warsaw Pact: Arms, Doctrine, and Strategy.* New York: McGraw-Hill Publications Co., 1982.

Liddell Hart, B. H. *The Classic Book on Military Strategy.* New York: Penguin Books, 1991.

Lowenstein, Prince Hubertus zu, and Volkmar von Zuhlsdorff. *NATO and the Defense of the West.* New York: Praeger Publishers, Inc., 1962.

Mattson, Maj Roy M. *Projecting American Airpower: Should We Buy Bombers, Carriers, or Fighters?* Maxwell AFB, AL: Air University Press, 1992.

Mearsheimer, John J. *The Tragedy of Great Power Politics.* New York: W. W. Norton & Company, Inc., 2001.

Miller, Lt Col D. M. O. et al. *The Balance of Military Power.* New York: St. Martin's Press, Inc., 1981.

Mitchell, William "Billy". *Winged Defense: The Development and Possibilities of Modern Air Power and Economic and Military.* Mineola, NY: Dover Publications, Inc., 1988.

Mueller, Karl. "Flexible Power Projection for a Dynamic World: Exploiting the Potential of Air Power." In *Holding the Line: U.S. Defense Alternatives for the Early 21st Century*, edited by Cindy Williams. Cambridge, MA: MIT Press, 2001.

Neufeld, Jacob. *Ballistic Missiles in the United States Air Force, 1945–1960.* Washington, DC: Office of Air Force History, United States Air Force, 1990.

National Defense Panel. *Report of the National Defense Panel on Transforming Defense: National Security in the 21st Century.* Arlington, VA: National Defense Panel, December 1997.

The National Security Strategy of the United States of America. Washington, DC: The White House, September 2002.

Neustadt, Richard E., and Ernest R. May. *Thinking in Time: The Uses of History for Decision Makers.* New York: Free Press, 1988.

Nye, Joseph S., Jr. *The Paradox of American Power: Why the World's Only Superpower Can't Go it Alone.* New York: Oxford University Press, 2002.

Paul, T. V. *Assymetric Conflicts: War Initiation by Weaker Powers.* New York: Cambridge University Press, 1994.

Pillsbury, Michael. *China Debates the Future Security Environment.* Washington, DC: National Defense University Press, 2000.

Schelling, Thomas C. *Arms and Influence.* New Haven, CT: Yale University Press, 1966.

Sherman, William C. *Air Warfare.* Maxwell AFB, AL: Air University Press, 2002.

Shlapak, David A., and Alan Vick. *"Check Six Begins on the Ground": Responding to the Evolving Ground Threat to U.S. Air Force Bases.* RAND, MR-606-AF, 1995.

Shlapak, David A., David T. Orletsky, and Barry A. Wilson. *Dire Strait? Military Aspects of the China-Taiwan Confrontation and Options for U. S. Policy.* RAND, MR-1217-SRF, 2000.

Shulsky, Abram N. *Deterrence Theory and Chinese Behavior.* RAND Corp., MR-1161-AF, 2000. RAND, 2000.

Slessor, J. C. *Air Power and Armies.* New York: Oxford University Press, 1982.

Sokolsky, Richard, Angel Rabasa, and C. R. Neu. *The Role of Southeast Asia in U.S. Strategy Toward China.* RAND, MR-1170-AF, 2000.

Steijger, Cees. *A History of United States Air Forces in Europe (USAFE).* Shrewsbury, UK: Airlife Publishing Ltd., 1991.

Stillion, John, and David T. Orletsky. *Airbase Vulnerability to Conventional Cruise-Missile and Ballistic-Missile Attacks: Technology, Scenarios, and U.S. Air Force Responses.* RAND, MR-1028-AF, 1999.

Stumpf, David K. *Titan II: A History of the Cold War Missile Program.* Fayetteville: University of Arkansas Press, 2000.

Swaine, Michael D., and Ashley J. Tellis. *Interpreting China's Grand Strategy: Past, Present, and Future.* RAND, MR-1121-AF, 2000.

Sun Tzu. *The Art of War.* San Francisco, CA: Westview Press, 1994.

Truman, Harry S. *Years of Trial and Hope.* Garden City, NY: Doubleday & Co., 1956.

Van Cleave, William R., and S. T. Cohen. *Tactical Nuclear Weapons: An Examination of the Issues.* New York: Crane, Russak & Company, Inc., 1978.

Vickers, Michael G., and Robert C. Martinage. *The Revolution in War.* Washington DC: Center for Strategic and Budgetary Assessments, 2002.

———. *Transforming the U.S. Military.* Washington, DC: Center for Strategic and Budgetary Assessments, 2001.

Walt, Stephen M. "Alliance Formation and the Balance of Power." In *The Perils of Anarchy: Contemporary Realism and International Security,* edited by Michael E. Brown, Sean M. Lynn-Jones, and Steven E. Miller. Cambridge, MA: MIT Press, 1995.

Periodicals, Articles, and Other Publications

Byman, Daniel, and Matthew Waxman. "Defeating US Coercion." *Survival* 41, no. 2 (Summer 1999): 107–20.

Campbell, Kurt M., and Derek J. Mitchell. "Crisis in the Taiwan Strait?" *Foreign Affairs* 80, no. 4 (July/August 2001): 14–25.

Christensen, Thomas J. "Posing Problems without Catching Up." *International Security* 25, no. 4 (Spring 2001): 5–40.

Friedberg, Aaron L. "The Struggle for Mastery in Asia." *Commentary* 110, no. 4 (November 2000): 17–27.

Gilboy, George, and Eric Heginbotham. "China's Coming Transformation." *Foreign Affairs* 80, no. 4 (July/August 2001): 26–39.

———. "Getting Realism: U.S. Asia (and China) Policy Reconceived." *The National Interest*, no. 69 (Fall 2002): 99–109.

Harrison, Selig S. "Time to Leave Korea?" *Foreign Affairs* 80, no. 2, (March/April 2001): 62–78.

Hawley, Gen Richard E., Michael B. Donley, and John R. Backschies. "Enhancing USAF's Pacific Posture." *Armed Forces Journal International* 140, no. 2 (September 2002): 54–56.

"ICBM Basing Options: A Summary of Major Studies to Define a Survivable Basing Concept for ICBMs." Office of the Deputy Undersecretary of Defense for Research and Engineering, December 1980.

Jumper, Gen John P., USAF. "Global Strike Task Force: A Transforming Concept, Forged by Experience." *Aerospace Power Journal* 15, no. 1, (Spring 2001): 24–33.

Moore, Frank W. "China's Military Capabilities." Cambridge, MA: Institute for Defense and Disarmament Studies, Policy Studies no. 2, June 2000.

Mueller, Karl. "Coercion and Air Power: A Primer for the Military Strategist." Paper presented at the Royal Netherlands Air Force Air Power Colloquium, Netherlands Defense Staff College, The Hague, 6 June 2000.

Mullins, Rob, and Laura Coco. "Prior and Current AF Thinking on Dispersed Operations." Slide Presentation. HQ/USAF, April 2001.

Pei, Minxin. "China's Governance Crisis." *Foreign Affairs* 81, no. 5 (September/October 2002): 96–109.

Rumsfeld, Donald. *Quadrennial Defense Review*. Washington, DC: Office of the Secretary of Defense, 30 September 2001.

Shambaugh, David. "Facing Reality in China Policy." *Foreign Affairs* 80, no. 1 (January/February 2001): 50–64.

Transforming Defense: National Security in the 21st Century. National Defense Panel Report. Arlington, VA: National Defense Panel, December 1997.

Warden, Col John A., III, USAF, retired. "The Enemy as a System." *Airpower Journal* 9, no. 1 (Spring 1995): 40–55.

Wohlstetter, Alfred, and Fred Hoffman. "Defending a Strategic Force after 1960." RAND: D-2270, 1 February 1954.

Interviews

Bowie, Christopher. Interview by author, 4 December 2002. School of Advanced Air and Space Studies, Maxwell AFB, AL.

Culp, Lt Col M. H., AMFE Director of Engineering. Interview by Dr. W. F. Sprague, USAFE Historical Division, Office of Information Services, 29 June 1955.

Ehrhard, Col Thomas. Interview by author, 22 April 2003. School of Advanced Air and Space Studies, Maxwell AFB, AL.

Grant, Rebecca. Interview by author, 21 October 2002. School of Advanced Air and Space Studies, Maxwell AFB, AL.

Hoster, Capt C. S., USAFE ODCS/Opns. Interview by Dr. W. F. Sprague, USAFE Historical Division, Office of Information Services, 28 June 1955.

Marshall, Andrew. Interview by author, 4 December 2002. School of Advanced Air and Space Studies, Maxwell AFB, AL.

Ochmanek, David. Interview by author, 16 October 2002. School of Advanced Air and Space Studies, Maxwell AFB, AL.

Vickers, Michael G. Interview by author, 4 December 2002. School of Advanced Air and Space Studies, Maxwell AFB, AL.

Unpublished Papers and Miscellaneous Documents

Air Force Quadrennial Defense Review. "Joint Freedom of Action: Defeating Anti-Access Strategies." USAF white paper. Washington, DC: USAF, May 2001.

Baker, Lt Col Coleman L. "Balancing the Equation: US Forces in Europe versus European Security." Student thesis, US Army War College, 1968.

Colella, Lt Col Robert A. "De-Ranged: Global Power and Air Mobility for the New Millennium." Maxwell AFB, AL: School of Advanced Airpower Studies, 2002.

Daniel, Maj Ronald E. "Strategy Comparison: Warsaw Pact." Maxwell AFB, AL: Air Command and Staff College, 1985.

"Global Engagement V." Post-Game Analysis draft concept paper, 2001.

O'Halloran, Maj Michael A. "A Kill is a Kill: Asymmetrically Attacking United States Airpower." Maxwell AFB, AL: School of Advanced Airpower Studies, 2000.

Stevens, Maj Charles A. "The European Military Environment." Maxwell AFB, AL: Air Command and Staff College, 1987.

Thompson, Maj Larry G. "The Quick Response Air Force: Decisive Expeditionary Airpower for the Future." Maxwell AFB, AL: School of Advanced Airpower Studies, 1996.

United States Air Force Historical Research Agency (AFHRA), Maxwell AFB, AL

Attachment to Memo for Col M.E. Marston. Subj: General Tunner's Summation of the Discussion Held at a Meeting. HQ USAFE, Main Conference Room, USAFE Dispersal Program, 29 December 1954.

Barton, Col Richard E., deputy chief of Strategic Air Command (SAC), DOOP. To SAC DOPL. "Alert Force Evaluation." In *History of SAC, Jan–Jun 58*, chap. II, vol. III. Internal SAC Headquarters Memo, 19 December 1957.

Bell, Col William J., USAFE ODCS/Opns. To commander, Twelfth Air Force. Subj: USAFE Dispersal Program. Letter, 8 December 1954.

Berdahl, Edgar O., HQ 2AF. "Comments on Reflex Action Based on Visit to Sidi Slimane, 23–27 Aug 57." In *History of 2AF, July–December 57.* Memo for Record, 23–27 August 1957.

Compton, Brig Gen K. K., Commander 5AD. To Maj Gen G. W. Mundy, Commander Second Air Force. In *History of SAC, Jan–Jun 58*, chap. 2, vol. 3. Letter, 1 October 1957.

Edmundson, Maj Gen J. V., DO. To Gen Thomas Power. "CINC Items on Northwest Trip." In *History of Strategic Air Command: June 1958–July 1959*, Historical Study 76, vol. VIII, 25 July 1958.

Fairchild, Col Frederic H. Acting chief, Plans Division of USAFE. To Brig Gen Royden E. Beebe, USAFE ACS/Opns. subj: Base Complex for Dispersal in France, 1 June 1954.

Headquarters Strategic Air Command. *History of Strategic Air Command, June 1958–July 1959*, Historical Study 76, vol. 1. SAC: Offutt AFB, NE, 1960.

———. *The SAC Alert Program, 1956–1959*, Historical Study No. Volume 1, 79. SAC: Offutt AFB, NE, 1960.

History of Headquarters United States Air Forces in Europe: 1 July–1 December 1954. Vol. 1. Office of Information Services Headquarters, Historical Division, USAFE, 1956.

History of Headquarters United States Air Forces in Europe: 1 January–31 December 1955. Vol. 1. Office of Information Services Headquarters, Historical Division, USAFE, 1956.

History. 305th Bombardment Wing (Medium), November 1957.

History. 306th Bombardment Wing (Medium), August 1957.

History. 3906th ABGp, July–December 1957. In *History of Strategic Air Command: June 1958–July 1959*, Historical Study 76, vol. VIII.

History. 3909th ABGp, May 1958.

HQ 2AF. "Report of TDY to Sidi Slimane." In *History of Strategic Air Command: June 1958–July 1959*, Historical Study 76, vol. VIII. Memorandum for record, July–December 1957.

HQ USAF. To all major commands. Subj: Vulnerability of Tactical Forces. Letter, 9 July 1954.

McConnell, Maj Gen J. P. To Gen Thomas D. White, chief of staff, USAF, "SAC Rotational Forces." In *History of Strategic Air Command: June 1958–July 1959*, Historical Study 76, vol. VIII, 4 October 1957.

Message. EOAC-7960. CINCUSAFE. To Commander 12th AF, 15 October 1954.

Message. EOOTS-T-5272. CINCUSAFE. To CINCUSAREUR and US CINCEUR, 3 August 1954.

Message. EOOTS-T-7084. CINCUSAFE. To US CINCEUR, 23 September 1954.

"Operation Reflex Action." In *History of SAC, Jan–Jun 58*, Chap. II, Vol. III. SAC memo, 12 June 1958.

Peaslee, Lt Col J. C., USAFE OACS/Opns, Plans Div. To USAFE ACS/Opns and COFS. Subj: NATO-USAF Officer Exchange; Report of Lt Col J. C. Peaslee. Letter, 2 July 1954.

Peterson, Arthur H. *VAPOR TRAIL–An Exercise in Dispersed Operation.* Headquarters USAFE Operations Analysis Report no. 1. Headquarters, USAFE: Germany, 14 March 1955.

Poage, Col Oren J. C/Temporary Dispersal Program Committee. To Col M. E. Marston. subj: Revision of USAFE Dispersal Program, 30 December 1954.

Ryan, Maj Gen J. D. To CINCSAC. "Overseas Staff Visit, 23 Oct–1 Nov 57." In *History of Strategic Air Command: June 1958–July 1959,* Historical Study 76, vol. VIII, 7 November 1957.

"SAC Air Operations Schedule (Peacetime)" and changes 1–4. In *History of Strategic Air Command: June 1958–July 1959,* Historical Study 76, vol. VIII, 1 May 1958.

Shy, Col W. M., Deputy Chief, Programs Division. "Review of SAC History." In *History of Strategic Air Command: June 1958–July 1959,* Historical Study 76, vol. VIII. SAC Memo, 19 December 1958.

Terrill, Maj Gen R. H., SAC DO. "Overseas Staff Visit, 27 Sep–12 Oct 57." In *History of Strategic Air Command: June 1958–July 1959,* Historical Study 76, vol. VIII. Report, 12 October 1957.

Trest, Warren A. *USAFE Dual-Based Forces, 1966–1973.* Office of History, HQ USAFE, 1974.

Tunner, Lt Gen W. H. To commander, Twelfth Air Force. Subj: Development and Implementation of Dispersed Operational Concept. Letter, 30 July 1954.

Uncles, Maj Gen John F., USA, USAREUR COFS. To CG Seventh Army. subj: Air Defense Planning. Letter, 29 December 1954.

USAFE Asst DCS/Opns. To 12th AF. subj: Selection of Bases for Development to Improve Dispersal Capabilities. Letter, 4 October 1954.

USAFE. "Program for Dispersal of Aircraft and Related Requirements, USAFE Tactical Bases, Germany, Fiscal Year 1955, DM Program." n.d. (1952).

———. *Chronology of the Cuban Missile Crisis, 6 October thru 24 November 1962.* USAFE, 1962.

———. "Reduction of USAFE Tactical and Logistical Vulnerability." USAFE, 15 January 1955.

USAFE Historical Monograph. *Air Force Posture in NATO's Central Region, 1947–1976.* Office of History, HQ USAFE: Ramstein Air Base, Germany, 1977.

USAFE Historical Monograph Series 1974, no. 3. *USAFE and the Commitment to NATO, 1949–1973.* Office of History, HQ USAFE, 1974.

USAFE Profile: Personnel Strength and Organizational Change, 1945–1985. Office of History, HQ USAFE, 1986.